CYCLING
NORWAY

From Trolltunga to Tromsø

D J ROBINSON

Table of Contents

About the Author

As of 2020, I work as a writer and editor, based in Barcelona. This book is part of the Island Rides project, for which my aim is to cycle 50,000 kilometres in 50 countries and to write a book about each. Although Norway is, of course, not an island, I would cross many along my way, especially in the north.

A percentage of profits from book sales is donated to charities local to the places I visit. In this case, the charity is the Norwegian Air Ambulance Foundation, an organisation providing emergency medical treatment throughout the country.

For pictures and videos from my trips, follow me on YouTube (DJRobinson_IslandRides), Instagram (Island_Rides), Strava (DJ Robinson), and Facebook (IslandRides1). (There are also some images at the back of the book.)

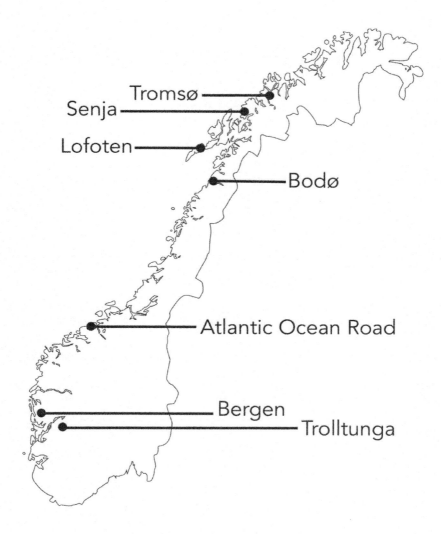

Tromsø

Senja

Lofoten

Bodø

Atlantic Ocean Road

Bergen

Trolltunga

Prologue

For a while, whenever I looked at a map of Norway, it felt like the first time. With a thousand fjords, a quarter of a million islands and even more lakes, learning Norway's shape is like memorising the arrangement of jumbled puzzle pieces. So intricate is the coast that if stretched into a straight line, it would span the equator. Twice. And then halfway again.

Even after a month there, I continued to learn things about Norwegian geography that astonished me. For example, Vardø, a town in the extreme northeast of the mainland, is further east than Istanbul! That Norway's northernmost point is also Europe's is less surprising. The desolate North Cape is the final destination for many cycle touring through Norway[1].

My starting point was Norway's second city, Bergen, the 'City of Rain', the wettest in Europe; enticed by the mountains of the southwest coast, clouds unload on Bergen on three out of every four days. My endpoint was Tromsø, the 'Capital of the Arctic'. Of the 4 million people that hang their hats in the Arctic Circle, 64,000 reside in Tromsø. It's the largest urban area in Northern Norway and the third largest anywhere on the wrong side of the 66th parallel north. Between mid May and late July, the sun never sets in Tromsø; between late November and mid January, it never rises.

I gave myself a month to cover the 2,000 kilometres between the two cities, starting in mid June and ending in mid July. I would camp along the way – in the wild as much as possible – and pass through a number of Norway's counties, whose names serve as chapter titles below: Hordaland, Sogn og Fjordane, Møre og Romsdal, Trøndelag, Nordland, and Troms.

Perversely, I would begin my south-to-north ride by heading southeast for several days. I had seen pictures of people on a tongue-shaped rock sticking out over an abyss, and concluded that I and my bike should inspect the structural integrity of said rock; if Trolltunga could withstand our combined weight and a few good stamps, I would declare it safe. Assuming this to be the case, the next stage would take me north and needlessly west to Atlantic Ocean Road, which winds across a scattering of skerries before ending in an underwater tunnel, off limits for cyclists. Not anticipating that I might tire of cycling by myself in the rain, I planned little for the subsequent 900 kilometres until I would reach the famed Lofoten Islands.

Fortunately, the roads to Lofoten became increasingly populated with other two-wheeled vagabonds whose steel frames had been drawn towards magnetic north from across Europe; their presence assured me I wasn't the only inhabitant of Earth to find wonder and awe in the pursuit of rolling slowly through the mystery of life; I came to feel, more and more, that I was part of something, a tradition that had long preceded me and would continue long after me. I was on the road north.

Hordaland

Har du røyka sokka dine?

Norwegian idiom meaning: 'Are you crazy?' Literal translation: 'Did you smoke your socks?'

It was on my first night that I realised camping wild for a month would be harder than I had imagined. After several hours on small roads and cycle lanes beside Bergen's highways – buying supplies at petrol stations, taking diversions around roadworks and feeling a little underwhelmed – I had slipped into a landscape of hills and lakes as the quiet of evening swept over the country. Spotting a rocky track, I went in search of my first wild campsite.

I descended the track until it split in two. One branch continued downwards, beside a stream, into a forest of bedraggled trees. I suspected that if I followed it, I would find myself at a private residence owned by knife-wielding thugs. There was of course no *reason* to think this, but think it I nonetheless did. The other branch led into a tunnel that disappeared into the side of a mountain. It seemed unlikely that it went anywhere, other than an abandoned mine, perhaps. It struck me as the type of place kids in a Stephen King novel would tell stories about. Stuck somewhere between thugs and monsters, I opted to take neither branch and to instead camp where I was.

Before setting up my tent, I wanted to do some work on my bike; it was a little bent out of shape from having been stowed in a soft bag during the flight, and since reassembling it I hadn't managed to get below fourth gear. So, next to the stream, I turned my bike upside-down and began poking it with tools.

That's when the creatures I would come to refer to as 'the little bastards' – more widely known as blackflies or, locally, as knotts – began to appear. They were at first dispersed in a wide cloud, like curious observers. But with every minute the pack became denser until my sweaty forearms were engulfed by the tiny insects and it seemed I was in a blizzard of black snow. I changed into longer clothing, put up the hood of my jacket and pulled the drawstring tight, though this only resulted in the flies concentrating their efforts on my face and eyes.

I swiped them away and, in the few seconds of visibility this granted, glanced despairingly at the track, through which grass and weeds grew, and at the entrance to the eerie tunnel. When the flies regrouped, I verbally pleaded with them to leave me alone, but to no avail. It crossed my mind that their eradication should become a primary focus for humanity, of at least equal importance to halting climate change and avoiding nuclear war.

Despite the flies, I managed to improve my gears slightly. I could now access second, as long as I held my thumb on the shifter. Eager to test this new-found gear on the hills and to leave the depressing little area I found myself in, I ditched my plan to spend the night by the track and headed back to the road. (It's lucky I made this decision when I did; according to a *Lonely Planet* article on Norway, 'the mental risks [of blackflies] can't be underestimated, as people have literally been driven insane by these ravenous hordes.')

I was rewarded for continuing with views of lakes, orange in the twilight, with little islands in them, some occupied by houses accessible by boat or bridge. I reached the town of Tysse, where a river poured into a fjord. It was almost midnight, but the sky was still pink and purple, like potpourri; the town's buildings, among them an old factory with a tall chimney, were silhouetted against molten-lava-coloured water.

The sides of the fjord were steep and any flat land had been claimed by houses, so finding somewhere to pitch was challenging. But it occurred to me that rivers often follow flat valley floors – nay, they *create* them – and that by heading upriver I might find somewhere to camp. Civil engineers had of course made similar observations, so there was a road beside the river and I cycled along it, enjoying the silence of the night. Between the road and the river was a broad, stony beach. Once well out of Tysse, I clambered down the bank to the beach and found a large, flat rock to pitch on. I stood still for a while. The only sound was the babbling of the river. Not a buzz, not a single little bastard in sight.

Norway's natural beauty continued to fill my eyes on my second day as I headed east, hoping to make it to Trolltunga within the next couple of days. The gentle river I had camped beside became a stampede of white water, cutting through tall brown cliffs, as I followed it up into the hills. At Fossen Bratte, the river becomes so mesmeric, falling 80 metres in a single leap, that in 1951 a honeymooning couple drove straight off the road and met their fate at the bottom of the deep valley. The afternoon sun tore through the clouds as I entered Norheimsund, a town on the edge of the ice-blue waters of Hardangerfjord, the second longest fjord in Norway and the fourth longest in the world at 179 kilometres. Amid the clanking of moored yachts and the squawking of gulls were the scents of sea salt and diesel.

On a quiet road on the north coast of the fjord, I amused myself by looking for wild camping spots, even though I wasn't ready to stop. To my immediate left were the almost-vertical flanks of 1,000-metre mountains; to my right, tall cliffs led down to the sea. I would occasionally spot stony beaches at the bottom of the cliffs, though they were of course inaccessible, and might soon be consumed by the tide, anyway.

As afternoon gave way to evening, I really did need to find somewhere to spend the night. I pulled over at the edge of the hamlet of Kvanndal, took a seat on my backpack and looked at my map. There was a ferry from Kvanndal to Utne, from where I could make my way towards Trolltunga. The famous rock was too far for me to reach that evening, so taking the ferry would mean finding somewhere to camp beside the road on the other side of the fjord. Since the road looked a lot like the one I was on, occupying a slither of land between mountains and water, my hopes of finding somewhere suitable were low. I also noted there were several long tunnels on the road near Utne and wasn't sure whether I was allowed through these on my bike and, if not, whether there were alternative routes. It crossed my mind that I might abandon my plan of seeing Trolltunga; it was a substantial detour, after all.

Unsure of what to do, I simply wandered into Kvanndal and immediately spotted a large campsite. In fact, the campsite essentially *was* Kvanndal. Other than the ferry terminal, there didn't seem to be much else. Since I'd originally planned to do so much wild camping, it was with some reluctance that I walked into the grounds of Kvanndal Camping on just my second night. I knew if I stayed in a campsite then, I wouldn't hesitate to do so again. In the café-cum-reception-cum-store, a tall old man stood behind the counter. I said *hei*, perused the shelves for comfort foods – crisps, croissants, bread, cheese, baked beans – then made my way to the till.

'Camping, too?' asked the man as he rang up my items.

'Yes, camping, too,' I confirmed.

Minus the food, I paid 100 kroner (US$10), which seemed very reasonable since I was in one of the most expensive countries in the world; on the previous day, I had been shocked to pay double that for a few bottles of water and some snacks from a petrol station.

Having checked in, after two full days on the road, I was excited to do things that are mundane in non-cycle-touring life, such as showering and cooking. With a plastic bag of delicacies swinging from my handlebars, I strode into the camp grounds past circles of wine-drinking retirees, got set up, then headed to the showers, where I revelled in the steamy water and watched the dirt and blood (I'd had a minor accident earlier in the day) slide from my skin and into the drain. Keeping an eye on the screen that said how many minutes I had left, I wished I had bought all the shower tokens in the world.

Refreshed, I retrieved my baked beans and entered the kitchen, only to find that it was being renovated and was presently nothing more than a dusty shell of a room. No microwave, no bowls, no spoons, no nothing. And so it was that, too tired to do anything else, I spent the second night of my heroic Norwegian adventure lying in my tent, watching a pirated version of *Pokémon Detective Pikachu* on my laptop and drinking cold beans from a can.

Having resolved to see Trolltunga, the next morning I rolled across the road to the ferry terminal. A lone car, filled by a family on holiday, occupied the expanse of concrete. The car rocked as the children played and the parents, their hair still dishevelled, stared stoically at the water, which was dull beneath the surrounding cliffs and the dark-grey duvet in the sky. Feeling not unlike the parents, I stood with my eyes closed as the terminal was gradually filled with the sounds of rumbling trucks and car radios. Whenever I opened my eyes, I saw that the ferry, at first a speck, had snuck a little closer, until it finally thundered to a stop in front of me, and I and the others filed on board.

The world became brighter as we left the cliffs of Kvanndal behind. A dozen mountain ridges, like the fins of mythical serpents, cut through the fjord. Their opacity seemed to diminish with distance, as if the furthest among them might just fizzle from existence. Pressing forward, the clouds thinned and light burst through, dancing with shadows on the surface of the water and igniting the white of snow-covered peaks.

'You're going to Trolltunga?' asked the ticket collector as we drifted towards the village of Utne, his finger on the button for the ship's bow visor.

'Yep, plan to get there tonight,' I told him, hoping he wouldn't inform me that the upcoming tunnels would be a problem.

He nodded. 'Well, a good day for it. A little windy, but a good day for it.'

I disembarked, spotting a couple on touring bikes arriving at the terminal from the direction I would go. Taking this as assurance that tunnels wouldn't be an issue, I began zipping down the coast. At times, the road was bordered by trees wrapped in luscious, green summer coats; at others, it passed apple orchards and red, wooden barns. There were tunnels, too, but when they were short I could ride through them and when they were long there were paths around them, revealing silent havens beside the fjord.

As I passed through Ednatunnelen, I saw daylight coming from a large crack in the wall on the other side of the road. I stopped, but couldn't make out what lay beyond, so checked for traffic then dashed across the lanes. Up close, I could see that a rocky path led outside. I left my bike and scrambled along it.

Ahead, I could hear the sound of running water. A couple of small trees grew from a patch of grass at the end of the path. Pushing aside the branches, I saw a pool of crystal water, several metres across, fed by a modest waterfall falling from the mass of grey rock that the tunnel cut through. The water must have come from the plateau above, where the Nordre Folgefonna glacier resides, a thousand metres up. Beside the pool and a section of level rock was an almost-vertical slope down which the glacial water ran into the jade surface of the fjord. Tiny cars on the other side of the fjord disappeared into tunnels, devoured by green mountains that burst from the water and into the sky.

To get a better idea of where I was, I clambered back into the tunnel to retrieve my drone, which transmits live images to my phone. I pointed the camera towards myself, then reversed over the fjord. I discovered that, a little to my left, there was another waterfall that began about 10 metres above me and that plummeted straight into the fjord, about 10 metres below. Reversing out further, another waterfall came into view. It dwarfed the other, being three or four times taller. Above it was an area of dark, lifeless rock, capped by an eternal snow that hinted at the frozen realm of the far-above plateau.

By early afternoon, I made it to Odda, a small town nestled in a valley at the southern tip of Sørfjord, a long, narrow branch of Hardangerfjord. It was Friday, but the weekend had come early to Odda, where cheers came from the cabins of moored boats and tourists drank in restaurant gardens, planning their hikes to Trolltunga or to the nearby glaciers.

I left town via a little bridge, which spanned a glassy river with grey stone banks, then began up the other side of Sørfjord. There were tunnels on this side too. Around the first was a path lined with trees, their yellow leaves like soft flames in the breeze. The next was a mile long and there was no way around it, but a small pavement meant I could distance myself from the traffic. When the tunnel ended, in the village of Tyssedal, the ascent to Trolltunga began.

It was a small and winding road. After thirty minutes I was drenched in sweat and realised I hadn't seen a single car or hiker heading my way, though there were plenty coming down. One fit looking couple grinned at me as we crossed paths. 'Wow, good luck!' they said.

At 400 metres up, the road flattened momentarily as it ran parallel to the steep banks of the river Tysse, then ended beside a lake and Skjeggedal car park, a popular starting point for those on their way to Trolltunga. I checked the map and saw that, to ascend the next 400 metres, I would have to take on a dozen tightly coiled switchbacks. This road, like the last, was paved, but was impossible to ride up with my 40-kilo loaded bike. So for the next hour I pushed it, stopping to rehydrate at every corner and nodding at perplexed-looking people coming down.

When the tarmac ended, the earth became more level and a trail of dirt and stone began. It wound through an expanse dotted with small trees and dissected by streams. The uneven surface meant I couldn't ride, but pushing was no problem and I assumed it would be like this the rest of the way.

Until I was stopped by a man on his way down.

He made a gesture I hadn't seen before. His fingers pointed towards his chest and his hand swivelled from side to side, flinging droplets of sweat onto the rocks. This meant nothing to me, I wanted to tell him, but there was something about his facial expression, a baring of his bottom-right teeth, that hinted at his meaning. *It's not a good idea, man.* He saw I didn't quite understand, so turned the way he'd come and pointed. In the distance, a path wound up a sharp ascent. Upon it, hikers plodded like weary ants.

I thanked the man for his warning, then continued, looking up at the incline to estimate how hard it would be. *Very hard, probably*, was the only conclusion I could draw as I edged towards it, but there was no turning back now.

Sadness washed over the face of the next man I encountered when he saw my bike, as if he'd just read a tragic headline. He removed his headphones to say one word, his pitch descending despairingly: 'Nooooooo!' One girl stopped dead and just stared. To break the silence, I asked whether it was far to the top. 'Uh, yeah!' she said, astounded by my naivety.

The reactions continued as I started up the steep section of the path, a staircase of hefty rocks embedded in loose earth. I heaved my laden bike to my shoulder, then climbed as many steps as my lungs would permit, a dozen or so per burst. After an hour of this, one man told me getting to the top with my bike was impossible. I looked back at the long trail below, which disappeared into a misty landscape of snow-capped mountains. I was starting to get frustrated with all the pessimism. *Can't he see how far I've already come?* I knew it would be hard, but as long as I could physically move, even if only metres at a time, surely I would get there eventually?

It was early evening when I reached a plateau and started along a mud path that ran beside small lakes formed from melting ice. My bike and I were now 1,000 metres above sea level and the path occasionally disappeared beneath swathes of snow. Everyone else was gone.

Dark clouds materialised and a cold rain began to fall. I put on my gloves and jacket. A red helicopter tore through the sky and I remembered reading about all the people that need rescuing from the Trolltunga trails each year. I started to question whether I had been too blasé about my little expedition. Maybe all the comments and stares of those coming down were justified. I reassured myself that if the weather worsened further I could set up my tent, put on some warm clothes and wait it out.

But the rain eased and the clouds dispersed. When I arrived at the end of the plateau, an immense blue lake, Ringedalsvatnet, came into view far below. It was filled by wisping waterfalls that fell from towering cliffs. The cliff tops were snow white, though the area around the lake was pine green. I recalled the most beautiful landscapes I had ever seen and nodded to myself: *yeah, this might take first place.*

The path became steep again. There were no steps this time, but I often picked up my bike to traverse boulders or to jump from one to another over streams. There were pre-existing bends, not part of the design, in my pannier rack, so I was diligent about setting my bike down softly after hauling it over obstacles, though less so as fatigue crept in. When one of the arms snapped, I hung a pannier from the handlebars and supported the rack with a bungee cord anchored to my saddle.

I thought the trail had finally got the better of me when I saw that an upcoming section was so steep that a rope had been laid across it and that the section began with a metre-high rock. Standing beside the rock, I waited a minute to rehydrate and to take a few deep breaths, then hauled my bike to my shoulder once again, wrapped the rope around a hand, and placed a foot on the edge of the rock. Pulling with every scrap of strength, I surmounted the rock, then dropped my bike back down. I waited for the dizziness to subside, then began up the muddy path, my feet sliding with every step.

As the path flattened out, I plodded on wearily, my head hanging over my chest, my eyes vaguely directed at the sludge below. I realised when I looked up that I had lost the red paint markers that led to Trolltunga. Setting my bike down, I trudged to the top of a mound to see where I was – near the edge of a cliff, beyond which were the lake and the waterfalls I'd seen hours before.

It was late evening. When the road had ended and the trail began, a sign indicated that I had 12 kilometres to go, and I expected that I would reach Trolltunga shortly. Six hours later, I was still some way away. I never saw Norway any darker than I did then; I was in the south and the pink of twilight had enveloped the surrounding white peaks. I had an inkling of which way to go, but had had enough for one day. I located a patch of flat ground between two pools of melted snow, set up my tent, and resolved to keep going in the morning.

A few hikers were already on the trail when I crawled out of my tent. To lighten my load, I left my tent and some things behind. I kept my bike with me, however; I was determined to join the ranks of the few foolish enough to bring a bike to Trolltunga, and to be the first to bring a touring bike there.

With less weight to carry and most of the elevation already gained, the beauty of the landscape eclipsed whatever pain I felt. I leapt between rocks surrounded by glimmering pools until, at last, Trolltunga came into sight, projecting from a cliff top and into a panorama comprised of distant waterfalls, unblemished peaks and the navy water of Ringedalsvatnet. It was the viewpoint to end all viewpoints.

I had met a local outside a supermarket the previous morning who had never been to Trolltunga. 'There are wonderful hikes everywhere here,' he said. 'Look around you!' He motioned towards an unbroken string of radiant mountains on the other side of the fjord. 'Hell, I hadn't even heard of that damn rock ten years ago!' While only a few hundred made the hike each year at the start of the millennium, 80,000 have every year since 2016, coinciding with a surge in the popularity of a certain social media app.

Being a user of said app, I handed my phone to a young Ukrainian guy when I arrived, then got in line to have my picture taken. It was barely midmorning, but already several people were waiting. My photographer forgot my passcode, so I shouted out the number when I reached the front of the line. A German girl, frustrated by how long this was taking, insisted that she and her entourage go ahead.

'Of course,' I said, stepping out of her way. *After all*, I thought, *rocks are fickle things. Better get your picture while you can.*

She looked at me suspiciously, pushed past, then began an elaborate choreography of poses with her friends. When they finished, I walked my bike to the tip of the tongue and sat with my feet over the edge, nothing but air below for 700 metres. I turned towards the Ukrainian, waved, hopped on my bike, then rolled back to the base.

I didn't hang around. The growing crowds, of which I was a part, diminished my sense of awe. It made me uneasy to see that majestic rock, who I imagined had enjoyed its previous solitude, treated as a mere stage for posing tourists. Besides, I still had to pick up my tent and start the hike back down.

After four more hours of lugging my bike, I made it back to the tarmac, then shot down to sea level like a runaway train, my handlebars quivering from the weight of the pannier they had adopted and my brake pads, now little more than strips of metal, threatening to combust. I needed to do some repairs.

A woman in Odda informed me it was Saturday afternoon and so the bike shop had of course already closed. It wouldn't open again until Monday[2]. I thought about continuing, but there wouldn't be anywhere else to buy bike parts for at least a few more days and I doubted the remaining arm of my rack would last much longer. So I decided to stay in Odda for the weekend.

I learned there was a campsite on the other side of town. Additionally, I learned the two ends of Odda are separated by a hill with a 15% gradient, up which I staggered, annoyed that the world's contours were indifferent to my exhaustion.

I pitched my tent next to a glassy lake cradled by steep mountains and fringed by pine. There were picnic benches beneath a shelter beside the kitchen, where I spent the cool, damp weekend recharging myself and my devices; I planned to sleep wild for a couple of nights after leaving Odda. I also mapped the 500-kilometre route to the next place on my to-see list: Atlantic Ocean Road.

On Monday morning, feeling rejuvenated and with a new pannier rack and brake pads, I sped back up the sunlit coast of Sørfjord, pleased to be heading north for the first time since beginning my ride to the Arctic. Occasionally, the road crossed silver rivers, fed by waterfalls that cascaded down the steep glacier-capped mountains beside the road. The water descended so quickly that at sea level it still held the chill of the summits above, a chill that I could feel rising from the rivers when I traversed them.

The campervans that had occupied the roads between Bergen and Trolltunga vanished as I crossed to the north of Hardangerfjord. The sun vanished too, and I rode into a grey and eerie silence and into a valley filled with malodorous farms, musty hay bales and rusting tractors. In the evening, I arrived at an abandoned lakeside cycling path covered with rocks and branches, pallets and old tyres. On the road, the quiet was interrupted only by the howls of trucks. Drizzle saturated the landscapes and washed away my sense of wonder. I considered stopping at a campsite in Myrkdalen, but the thought of being stationary in this bleak world was less appealing than edging through it. The heavens punished my persistence, releasing a torrent that audibly pummelled my jacket as I began an ascent, where I watched the road's white lines creep by. *Fine*, I responded to the sky, *I'll look for somewhere to stop.*

I scoured the landscape, but any morsel of flat land had been snatched up by houses and farms. Creaking onwards, the hope I might come across an uncultivated plain was dashed by a sign welcoming me to a ski resort. Further on, the resort, houses and farms were replaced by forests that sprang from slithers of flat, rain-soaked ground. Exhausted and realising I was unlikely to find anywhere better, I ventured into a boggy woodland. I lay my bike against a tree and began searching for somewhere to pitch, pressing the soft earth with my feet to see how far they would sink. When I found a patch of land where the water only covered the top of my shoes, I decided it would have to do.

Inside my tent, I changed into jeans, a t-shirt, a hoody and a jacket; I had learned on my first night in Norway that layers were necessary to stay warm through the night. I spread my riding clothes across my bags, overly optimistic that they might be slightly less soaked by the morning. Lying on my inch-thick air mattress — which would be flat before the morning due to a puncture — I listened to the rain fall on the nylon and slapped together some bread and sliced cheese. Images of the day's ride — the fjords, the farmland, the forlorn cycle paths — drifted through my mind as I stared at the ceiling, lit as always by a sun that never set though was seldom seen. Having left behind Hardanger, famed for its fjords and for Trolltunga, I wondered if the prior few hours of sodden fields foreshadowed the rest of the trip. Also, I hadn't seen a single cyclist since leaving Hardangerfjord and imagined myself drifting through the mist for weeks on end, encountering nobody with whom to share my journey.

But for the first time in Norway I had covered over 100 kilometres in a day, the distance I hoped to reach most days going forward. Despite my apprehensions, I was pleased to have taken my first chunk out of the south-north axis.

Hordaland Statistics

- Distance: 355 kilometres

- Climbing: 5,722 metres

- Highest point: 1,212 metres (Trolltunga)

- Island Rides project distance: 2,839 kilometres

- Island Rides project climbing: 25,605 metres

Sogn og Fjordane

It was still murky in the woods near Myrkdalen as I climbed out of my tent in the morning. In the cold of the drizzly dawn, my muscles involuntarily tensed as I plodded around my tent, retrieving pegs from the soggy ground. Emerging from the trees wearing clothes still soaked by yesterday's rain, I planted my feet on the road and hoped for an incline to raise my temperature.

At the end of a dark green valley, where cows and sheep grazed in the mist, I got what I wished for; the valley's river was fed by two large waterfalls that descended from a plateau, accessed by a series of switchbacks. As the rising road warmed me up, I rewarded myself at every hairpin with a 30-second breather and a few gulps of Norway's answer to Fanta No Sugar, the superiorly named Solo Super. On occasion, the sun poked his head through small blue windows in the sky.

'Shall I come out?' he asked.

'Yes, I would love you to!' I responded.

'I bet you would, wouldn't you?' he said smugly.

'Yes,' I replied. *Wasn't that clear?*

'Shall I do it? Shall I come out, then?'

'Definitely, that'd be great,' I confirmed. *What's with this guy?*

'Hmm.'

'You're unsure?' I asked.

'Yeah, I'm not sure… what month is it, by the way?'

I informed him that it was June. 'It's basically summer.'

'Hmm,' he responded hesitantly.

'Please.'

'Naaaah.'

'No?'

'Naaaah.' he said again, 'but I'll be back soon.'

After the switchbacks, an icy wind awaited me on the desolate plateau, through which the Hordaland-Sogn og Fjordane county line runs. The cold seeped back into my bones. I crawled past grey, trembling lakes and snow-covered slopes. As I reached the far edge of the plateau, a heavy rain began, needling my eyes on what would otherwise have been a rapturous 15-kilometre descent to a fjord-side town. I was shivering as I arrived in Vikøyri, and made my way to the shelter of a petrol station where I replenished my stock of Solo Super and bought two coffees, one to drink and the other to warm my unoccupied hand.

I continued to shake as I followed the coast of Sognefjord – the so-called King of Fjords, the longest (205 kilometres) and deepest (1,308 metres) in Norway – to Vangsnes ferry terminal. Beside the small line of cars and campervans was a heated bathroom where I hid out, running hot water over my hands. When the ferry arrived, I was delighted to find a wastefully warm lounge with cushioned seats and radiators beneath every window.

On the other side, the road was flanked by dandelions, purple foxgloves and young pines. Beside the road, emerald waters lapped at rocks adorned with bright yellow seaweed. The rain stopped, but the perpetual sound of descending water soaked the atmosphere; with Norway's omnipresent cliffs and talent for seducing clouds, it was only in rare spots that I couldn't count a handful of waterfalls. With little traffic, the only sound was the soothing static of the water.

At the northern tip of Vetlefjord – a branch of Fjærlandsfjord, itself a branch of Sognefjord – I entered a valley of farmland and silver birch. At the end, the road looped upwards to 700 metres. After two hours of continuous climbing up into the clouds past suspicious families of sheep, I arrived at the elaborate Gaularfjellet viewing platform. This triangular concrete structure juts out into empty space, from where you can admire imposing dark mountains in the distance, blankets of pine and the curving of the road you've conquered.

As I did just this, it began to rain, so I made my way across the empty car park to a sheltered area beside the public toilets, where I regarded my surroundings and considered how much further I should go before calling it a night. The road had climbed higher than I had expected and patches of snow clung to the damp, grassy slopes. Moreover, I wasn't yet at its crest and I began to imagine that, if I continued, I would find myself on top of a rain-swept mountain, desperately scouring the landscape for tent-sized patches of dry ground.

Or I could spend the night here, I thought, peering into the spacious bathroom. Sure, it smelled and there were urine stains on the concrete floor, but as public bathrooms go, it wasn't too shabby and would be warmer than my tent. I was, however, hesitant. I envisioned lying in my sleeping bag, tensely listening to the angry banging on the door of a man with an upset stomach; creepy eyes peering through the panel of glass that ran along the top of the wall; the lock turning – *someone has a key!* – and then a cleaner screaming upon discovering a wide-eyed cyclist hiding in the darkness.

It was now mid-evening and, convinced that it was unlikely anyone would be visiting this mountaintop car park before I began my cycle of shame in the morning, I pushed my bike into the bathroom and locked the door.

Once I'd relaxed a little, I was pleased to not go through the process, simple though it was, of putting up my tent and of removing my bags from my bike; it was a luxury to simply lean my bike against a wall and take from my panniers whatever I needed. I started with my air mattress, the head of which I positioned beneath the sink, ensuring my nose would be as far from the toilet as possible. Next, I laid my sleeping bag on top of the mattress and got changed into my night-time clothes. The final step was to turn out the light; since there wasn't a switch, this meant hanging my rain jacket over the motion sensor which projected from the wall above the toilet.

I was drifting off when a vehicle pulled into the car park. My eyes shot open. There were the sounds of a car door shutting, a man coughing and then approaching footsteps. I stared up at the door handle, waiting for it to move. I pictured the man outside, annoyed and confused to find the middle-of-nowhere toilet locked. But the handle didn't move; he used the adjoining bathroom. After, he stood beneath the shelter outside the toilets, smoking and burping, then walked back to his car and drove off.

In the early hours of the morning, there were more noises outside. This time they came not from a human but from a posse of bell-wearing sheep, which clomped around just outside the door, baaing at their friends across the valley.

Once they had departed, I slept an hour or two more, before being woken by the sound of the door handle, followed by a woman's voice.

'Hello?' came the voice.

Damn, I thought, *that must be the cleaner. The game's up!* I returned her hello, then got up to unlock the door, but she beat me to it.

When the door swung open, I saw a robust woman wearing a military-green jacket and blue jeans. Before I could explain myself, she entered the room. I half expected her to start throwing my things through the doorway, so was pleasantly surprised when she spoke in a sweet voice, in an accent I learned was Latvian.

'I be quick. Ten minutes maximum,' she said. 'It's four in the morning.' She didn't want to be there any longer than she had to.

As she set about replacing the paper towels and toilet rolls (after I had removed my jacket from the motion sensor), we talked a little about where we were from and about my trip.

'People sleep here regular,' she said, which perplexed me. Other than other touring cyclists, of which I'd seen very few, I couldn't imagine who else might stay there.

I slept a little more after she left, though my woolly friends soon made their return, stamping their hooves and ringing their bells, so at seven I reluctantly packed up and put my cycling shorts back on.

Continuing, I was pleased to find I had almost reached the high point of the road (784 metres) the previous night, so after just a short climb a long descent began. The sheep that had kept me awake fled when they saw me coming, running in a straight line down the road for minutes at a time before it finally dawned on them to turn onto the adjoining steep banks of grass and rock. The road wound downwards through forests of birch and pine, following a river that disappeared into and reappeared from a series of lakes.

The descent ended in the sleepy town of Vic, after which I couldn't find much joy in riding. Despite stocking up on my staples – bread, cheese, apples, crisps and Solo Super – my energy dwindled as I entered the surrounding farmland. Tractors were busy spreading manure or carrying steaming heaps of it along the roads in trailers, and the smell was overpowering. I tried to breathe through my mouth, using my clenched teeth as an air filter, but only ended up with the taste of dung in my throat. Also, the commotion in the fields upset the local flies, which retreated in swarms to the roads; often they found their way into my eyes, requiring me to stop and scoop them out with a dirty finger. By evening, I was creeping along the shore of a 30-kilometre lake. The endless turning of my legs felt painfully monotonous.

As I neared the end of the lake, I spotted a campsite on the other side. It was still early, though I needed to rest and to somehow reignite my enthusiasm. I set up beside the water, then took a seat in the campsite's empty kitchen and began poring over maps, searching for inspiration. It occurred to me that cycling was feeling tedious as I wasn't giving myself anything to look forward to. I decided that each day I should identify something I would like to see. Most of the attractions I'd pass the next day involved skiing or traversing glaciers – neither easy with a bike – but there was an old wooden church in the village of Olden, a few hours away. This didn't exactly thrill me, but I liked the idea of splitting my day in two.

Looking at maps also gave me a chance to see how I was progressing. I calculated that if I took the most direct route from where I was, the village of Skei, to Tromsø via Atlantic Ocean Road and Lofoten, never straying off course or taking a rest day, I would need to average 86 kilometres per day to make my flight home. That didn't sound too bad until I worked out that during my first week in Norway I had averaged just 65. Kilometres aside, it was clear from a glance at the map that I still had a very long way to go; despite my fatigue and aching knees, the tiny section of map between Bergen and Skei was a mere eighth of the distance from Bergen to Tromsø. But with no more Trolltunga-scale excursions planned, I felt confident that I could make up for my slow start.

The next morning I included in my shopping a litre of chocolate milk to be used as a mood stabiliser; by drip feeding myself a sugary drink throughout the day, I thought I might avoid slumps in energy and maintain my morale. Additionally, I bought a large bag of trail mix comprised of nuts, raisins and chocolate; I had discovered previously that this particular salty-sweet combination was one of the best things that can happen to a mouth, so hoped regular handfuls would also contribute to sustaining my spirits.

This treat-based approach to happiness was at first successful. The day's ride began with a main road which I hadn't been eager to ride, the 1,300-kilometre E39. However, once on it, I stopped noticing the traffic as I realised that in each ostensibly generic Norwegian landscape there is something that sets it apart. In this case, it was the colour of the Stardalselva river, whose aquamarine waters wound beside the road, luminous beneath the grey sky. As I approached the spot where I would turn off, the river poured into a lake of the same colour, nestled between mountains of dark pine. I sat on a picnic bench beside it, humbled by the beauty.

Alas, at the village of Byrkjelo I left the water behind to ascend a 600-metre ridge, draped in dreary farmland. As I neared the top over an hour later, I rammed my thumb into the shifter, pleading with it to give me first gear, though succeeded only in getting the chain stuck between the cassette and spokes.

I tried to extract it with brute force, turning my hands black and red in the process, but it wouldn't budge. To enable yanking from different angles, I removed the wheel, requiring that I also remove my new rack, whose long bolts prevented access to the axle nuts. I yanked away again, still to no avail. Inspecting the problem more closely, I saw that one of the chain's pins was lodged into a groove on the inside of first gear; it wasn't going to move, no matter how hard I pulled. After half an hour, during which an assembly of flies came to oversee the operation, I had the idea of using a long screwdriver to lever the chain sideways, releasing the pin from the groove. With one hand on the screwdriver, I used the other to pull the chain, which eventually slid out from behind the gears.

All that remained was to put everything back together. Since the rack wasn't a great fit for my frame and since my panniers weren't a great fit for the rack, this required more time and bending of things than it should. Eventually, however, I got them back on, then just needed to reconnect the brake. Normally, this only takes a few seconds, but my bike seemed determined to test me. I squeezed the brake arms together as hard as possible, yet couldn't get the cable back in place. Luckily, I had a solution: I unleashed an onslaught of physical and verbal abuse upon my bike, furiously kicking it from every angle and imploring it to understand the depths of its inadequacy. How I ultimately solved the brake problem, I don't recall.

When I arrived at the top of the ridge, two hours after starting the ascent, I was greeted by a charming plateau, where sheep plodded and clouds drifted across the grassy slopes of a ski resort, closed for summer. I then began a winding descent on which I picked up so much speed that a car pulled over to let me pass. Next, the road followed the coast of Innvikfjord, where at the end of a closed lane I met a pleasant old man whose job was to hold one of those signs with green on one side and red on the other. Until the call came to turn the sign, we talked about my days ahead. He proudly reported that he'd recently finished a job on Atlantic Ocean Road, controlling traffic while a car chase was filmed for the upcoming James Bond movie.

By late afternoon, I arrived in Olden, the location of the church I had decided to visit. Having been slowed by bike troubles, I was tempted not to bother, but it wasn't much of a deviation so I kept to the plan.

The wooden church, handsome and red, stood in the grassy outskirts of the village. I leant my bike against a fence, walked up to the heavy door and pushed it open. I stepped lightly as I made my way in, half expecting to be ambushed by a priest, though there was nobody there. The aisle led to three small stained-glass windows under which hung a painting of Jesus glancing serenely upwards, guarded by Roman soldiers. Admiring the organ up on the mezzanine and the scarlet cushions on the pews, I was struck by how pristine everything was, as if nobody had ever set foot inside the 85-year-old church other than to dust or polish. Likewise, the grass in the cemetery, where neat flowers adorned granite graves, was freshly mowed. An elderly woman with a bag of gardening tools hobbled in as I headed back to my bike. I watched her kneel beside a grave and tend to plants.

For the next hour, I followed the coast of Innvikfjord. Moored in Olden, population 500, was the cruise ship *MV Ventura*, population 3,000. For the passengers who occupied the countless balconies of the colossal vessel, a local band played on a stage beside a restaurant. Sometime after leaving Olden behind, I heard the ship honk its appreciation, its deep horn filling the fjord. I then passed an artificial sandy beach tucked into a cove. Like the ship, it seemed out of place, especially with the dark skies and rain starting to fall. I sheltered for a while beneath a pedestrian bridge, watching the thickening haze above the water. When I continued, there were occasional breaches in the clouds and a radiant gold would pour from the heavens onto the shadowy surface of the fjord.

When I left Innvikfjord, I was just 20 kilometres from Grodås, my target for the day, and fully expected to make it there. On the other side of Stryn, one of the larger towns on the fjord, trucks roared past as the road turned inland and upwards. After cresting the hill, I began a fast descent towards a lake (Hornindalsvatnet, the deepest in Europe). Still the trucks tore past, ripping the moisture from the road and flinging it into the air. When my rear axle snapped on a quiet bridge at the bottom of the hill, my irritation was accompanied by relief. Had it given out a minute earlier, I might have lost control at speed and amongst traffic.

It was mid evening and I was still some way from Grodås, so the possibility of locating a mechanic was remote; all I could do was continue on foot and try find somewhere to sleep.

After I while, I arrived at the start of a dark and narrow tunnel that cut through a headland. Since I now took up more space than usual, walking beside my bike, and there were still a few trucks around, the tunnel seemed a perilous way forward, so I looked for an alternative route.

Beside the road, next to the lake, was a lumber yard. The corrugated iron roofs of the shacks were covered in rust, though the piles of freshly cut planks suggested the yard was still in use. Beyond it was a path that followed the edge of the headland. I crossed the road and walked to the start of a gravel track that led down to the yard, where there was a simple gate – just a plank laid on top of two wooden posts – and a red sign prohibiting entry. At this point, I noticed a black dog scampering about amongst the piles of planks and sawdust. When it spotted me, it sprinted up the track. I prepared to defend myself but it gave me a wide berth then sheepishly ran across the road, disappearing down the driveway of a lonely white house hidden among the trees.

After removing and replacing the plank at the yard's entrance, I walked slowly into the grounds. I scrutinised the shacks for life, but there was none. At the start of the path that followed the headland was another gate, easy enough to walk around, and another red sign. I plodded along the path, following a bank that led to a grey-stone beach scattered with neglected dinghies. Despite a certain eeriness, I suspected the path might lead to an idyllic wild campsite.

And it did. The tip of the headland was a triangle of rich earth that extended into the grey-blue waters of the lake, fringed by rocks and dotted with pine and small plants. Unable to see Grodås or hear the road leading there, I set up next to the water and let the gentle lapping sounds wash over me as I drifted off to sleep.

I continued my stroll in the morning. The path to the other side of the headland was blocked in places by piles of large rocks that had tumbled from a cliff. Someone had spray painted upward-facing arrows on one of the piles (lest people try to burrow beneath them). I heeded their advice and hoisted my bike to my shoulder, then staggered over. At the end of the path was another gate; on the outside of this one was a sign of a stick man about to be splattered by an avalanche of rocks. This was clearly the reason for the way being closed.

From there, Grodås was just a few kilometres down the road. After a visit to tourist information, which was not an office but a notice board in a car park, and consulting supermarket and hotel staff, it was established that I should go back to Stryn, where there was a bike shop. The receptionist at the hotel instructed me to wait behind the petrol station where a bus bound for Oslo would arrive at 11.43. When it did, I stowed my bike below, climbed into the warmth, and settled into a soft seat, where I fantasised about ditching my bike and riding buses to Tromsø instead.

I was fighting to keep my eyes open as we pulled into Stryn. I alighted and lumbered onwards, past cafes and outdoor clothing outlets, to the bike shop. When I presented my wheel to the young mechanic and told him the axle had broken, he stared at it intently. I waited for him to propose a solution, though he simply concurred that it was broken, then disappeared into a workshop.

As well as bikes, the place sold an array of camping and hiking gear, which I perused to pass the time, concealing from onlooking staff my disbelief at the prices. Whenever I tired of this, I'd poke my head into the workshop and ask how it was going. My young friend would give me some technical explanation of what he was doing and I'd pretend to understand. The essential problem, however, was that my wheel was so cheap and out of date that it was incompatible with the parts the shop stocked.

I went to a restaurant for a pizza, then checked in on the situation again. Still the mechanic was staring at my broken wheel, but seeing me seemed to spark a revelation. With a distant stare that suggested the recollection of something long forgotten, he exited the workshop and made for the bikes on the shop floor. He scanned each of them as he walked – *not this one; no, not this one either* – until he reached the one he'd been looking for. Wiping dust off the saddle, he told me it was the worst bike in the shop and, as such, its wheel might be compatible with mine. He removed the wheel, dropped the frame with contempt, then headed back to the workshop to see if it would fit.

I went back to perusing the wares, confirming that rain covers for backpacks would require a small bank loan. As I began to consider napping in a hammock, the mechanic reappeared with my bike and confirmed that he'd replaced the wheel.

At the till, I thanked him for his work, but he seemed reluctant to acknowledge my gratitude. Perhaps he knew the wheel wouldn't last long.

Sogn og Fjordane Statistics

- Distance (trip total): 301 kilometres (656 kilometres)

- Climbing (trip total): 4,145 metres (9,867 metres)

- Highest point: 988 metres (Stølsheimen Nature Preserve)

- Island Rides project distance: 3,140 kilometres

- Island Rides project climbing: 29,750 metres

Møre og Romsdal and Trøndelag

'I love three things,' I then say. 'I love a dream of love I once had, I love you, and I love this patch of earth.'

'And which do you love best?'

'The dream.'

From *Pan* by Knut Hamsun, Norwegian writer

I awoke the next morning in Hellesylt, a village at the southern tip of Storfjord. Beyond the damp grass of the campsite, walls of rock pierced the clouds and towered over the dark blue water. I could see the road north ascending a steep hill on the edge of the village before being swallowed by the cliffs. This meant I would soon be swallowed by them, too. I had been in Norway a week, in this country of endless mountains where often the only way forward is to bore through Earth's guts. Still, tunnels made me uneasy.

I thought back to my second day when I had shot through a series of short tunnels as part of a winding descent, imagining myself as a pod-racing Anakin Skywalker swooping among the canyons of Tatooine. The driver of a thunderous old truck evidently saw me differently and hovered behind as we plummeted, alternating between daylight and darkness. A cyclist had recently been killed in a tunnel on this very road, so I urged myself to be cautious and to let the truck pass.

As we neared the end of one tunnel, I spotted a lay-by just outside. Not yet used to the weight of my loaded bike, the steep, descending bank on the far side of the lay-by approached more quickly than expected. I pulled my brakes harder. My tyres skidded over some loose stones and I was flung to the ground. As I floundered there, weighed down by my backpack, the truck slunk past.

More embarrassed than hurt, I got to my feet, dusted myself off and continued. Then I heard a beep behind me. A car, heading the other way, had stopped at the entrance to the tunnel. I thought it strange but wasn't about to go back uphill to investigate. When the car pulled up beside me at the bottom of the descent, at first I didn't recognise it. The driver, a portly, older man in a Hawaiian shirt, wound down his window. He had seen me fall and come to see if I was OK. Touched, I assured him I was and thanked him for checking. 'You're certain?' he asked, nodding towards my leg. I glanced down. My right knee was now devoid of skin and my shin coated in blood.

Despite passing through 70 of Norway's 1,000 or so tunnels during my trip, I never shook the feeling that there's something chilling about them.

Firstly, there's often a literal mountain's worth of rock above; if even a fraction fell on you, it would, of course, be game over but what scared me more was the possibility that, by some unfortunate miracle, the falling debris might somehow miss my head and vital organs, and I'd be pinned by rubble to the frigid concrete with no way out.

Secondly, there's the disorientating way sound travels. It seems to flow backwards and forwards and to compound indefinitely. On more than one occasion, I braced myself for the hurricane that would follow what was certainly an 18-wheeler, only to be passed by a pensioner on a scooter.

Lastly, there's the prospect of being hit by a car. Assuming you have lights, the width of the tunnel is what most affects your chances of becoming overly familiar with someone's tyre tread. When wide, tunnels in

Norway often have pavements, providing cyclists with their own lane, separate from the traffic; when narrow, they don't, and you might be forced to call upon your inner tightrope walker as you wobble along a grit-covered sliver of concrete between the cold walls of the tunnel and the discernibly hot engine of an overtaking car.

Knowing that tunnels can be survival-prohibitive for cyclists, the Norwegian authorities have declared a large proportion of them off limits to anyone not in a vehicle. In many cases, this is because their length would result in prolonged exposure to fumes. Lærdal Tunnel, for instance, the longest road tunnel in the world at almost 25 kilometres, might take a tortoise-like cyclist such as myself a couple of hours to pass through.

For many of the tunnels that cyclists aren't allowed through, there are paths that go around them, often following the edge of a fjord. I always looked forward to these; they were a chance to get away from any traffic and to explore little fragments of Norway that few others see. Moreover, they varied so much in their quality that I never knew what I'd find. There might be mowed lawns, waterside picnic benches and a sense that tending to the path is routinely added to the local council's to-do list, or, commonly – and these are the sort I found more interesting – there might be makeshift gates that suggest you go no further, a swirl of branches, tyres and pallets, and a sense that long ago, the council discreetly erased the path from their maps. Such paths make use of old roads that, with advances in tunnel making, were abandoned due to their proclivity for amassing large piles of rocks.

I continued to gaze at the road out of Hellesylt as I stood outside a supermarket, drinking coffee from a paper cup and blowing steam into the morning air. To put off riding, I read about where I was. I learned there was once a ferry between Hellesylt and Stranda, the next village I would pass through, 30 kilometres up the coast of Storfjord, on the other side of some big hills and tunnels. From the computer-translated article, I couldn't figure out when the ferry had stopped running, though there was something about 1937, so it seemed I'd missed the last voyage by some time and that there would be no getting out of riding.

The road to Stranda began with an uphill tunnel, about four kilometres in length. As trucks rumbled past, I wobbled along a narrow pavement, skirting around lights and SOS phone booths extending from the tunnel wall. Protected from the elements and climbing continuously, I started to sweat. When I reached the end of the tunnel, 30 minutes after entering it, I was down to shorts and a t-shirt. Coaches were parked in a small car park overlooking the fjord, now several hundred metres below, and dozens of tourists, all bundled in winter clothing, turned away from the snowy mountains they had come to admire, to smile at me and wave and to rub their arms, feigning cold. I wiped the sweat from my brow and waved back. It began to rain as I descended through the windswept valley to Stranda and I was again wrapped in layers as I rolled into a ferry terminal.

On the other side of Storfjord, I headed inland. Once the cars from the ferry had all overtaken me, I had the road to myself. However, the ferry would soon bring the next load of cars and there was a tunnel approaching and my rear light had begun to misbehave, turning itself off without warning. There was silence as I was enveloped by the darkness. I kept my ears pricked for the sound of traffic and pedalled hard. Near the exit, the hum of cars began to reach me, increasing in volume until one car shot past, the driver with their hand pressed on the horn. I pulled over as I re-entered daylight, gulped some water, and confirmed that my light was no longer on. The road continued upwards for a while, then turned and descended to the fjord-side town of Stordal. Like many settlements in Norway, Stordal, with its sprawling fields and red wooden barns, wouldn't have seemed out of place in the American Midwest, if not for the surrounding cliffs and waterfalls.

The map showed another long tunnel after Stordal, but also a small coastal road parallel to it. It started as a smooth single lane, then gradually narrowed and deteriorated until it was a mere strip of warped asphalt, its flanks hidden beneath thick layers of decaying foliage. Weeds and long grass had pierced the slither of bare surface. I weaved between scattered rocks and ducked under the branches of overhanging trees. It turned out this road also led to a tunnel.

Abandoned for two decades, there was a metal fence at its entrance, though like the road, its shape had been distorted by time and, had I been inclined, I could have walked right in. Of course, I was not inclined, so just stared for a while into the darkness of the forgotten tunnel, listening to the echoes of unseen drips.

A path went around it, occupying a thin section of land next to and some way above the fjord. Overgrown and contorted, the path was much like the so-called road. Slowly, I cycled along it for several minutes, hoping I would soon reach the other end, but I never got that far. A landslide had blocked the way and a head-high pile of rocks extended as far as I could see. I might have been tempted to clamber over them, had they not been so close to a long drop to the fjord.

As I re-joined the main road where I'd left it, grey mountains were visible across the fjord. I imagined colossal chunks of them sliding silently into the water, the light reaching me before the sound. By the time I heard the rumble, great waves would have arisen. Hungry for human life, they would race towards the shores, where they'd crush homes as if they were made from matches. In 1731 and in 1934, this really happened. On both occasions, millions of cubic metres of rock plunged into Storfjord. Waves up to 64 metres high galloped through the darkness, engulfing entire villages. During the first of these tsunamis, one family made it to the roof of their farmhouse, but the roof detached itself and they floated out into the fjord. It was January, the coldest month of the year. By the morning, the family's five children had frozen to death. As of 2019, a mountain overlooking the water near Hellesylt is one of the most closely monitored in the world. Each year, a 700-metre crack grows a little more, threatening to release 130 million tonnes of rock into the fjord.

The remaining stretch to Vestnes began with Stordal Tunnel, which I had tried to avoid by taking the overgrown coastal road. It was long and damp and I virtually slid through it, balancing on a mud-covered strip between the tunnel wall and the traffic. In contrast, an idyllic fjord-side road went around the next tunnel, north of Dyrkorn. Although off limits to cars, it had been kept in perfect condition and was enjoyed by strolling locals, including a couple with Scandinavian-blonde hair and their elated Pomeranian. Later, there was a T-junction and signs pointing in opposite directions. Since leaving Trolltunga, Alesund had been the 'major' settlement to the north[3]. I realised that I was now at the same latitude as Alesund and, for the first time, didn't follow the sign that pointed in its direction; the next big settlement to the north was Trondheim, a few days away. The road to Trondheim began with an hour-long climb, during which it started to rain. I counted my pedal strokes, allowing myself a swig of Solo Super each time I reached 500.

I coasted into Vestnes in the late afternoon and looked for somewhere to replenish my supplies. A white-haired man approached me in the supermarket car park, plastic bags swaying in his fingertips. 'You're doing a cycle tour?' he asked.

I confirmed that I was and outlined my ride: flew from London, started riding in Bergen, headed to Tromsø. He said he'd once flown to London, bought a bike then cycled to Newcastle before taking an overnight ferry home.

We talked about ferries in Norway. 'They're the best part of my day,' I told him.

He smiled knowingly. 'Yes, but they used to be much nicer. More attractive and welcoming. These days they all look like amphibious landing vehicles.'

I took a moment to appreciate his knowledge of obscure English, then ventured that, regardless, it was probably nicer to take a ferry across a fjord than to drive beneath one.

'I agree,' he said. 'Wholeheartedly. But the government wants to do away with all the ferries. Wants to replace them all with more tunnels. It'll cost billions. And they're not safe. The fjords are so deep that the roads into them have to be very steep. Too steep for the trucks. It's not unusual for heavy vehicles to catch on fire, what with all the braking. And there're plans to build a floating tunnel across Sognefjord. The first in the world, I think. A terrorist's dream, if you ask me.'

We spoke for a while; he was in Vestnes visiting family and didn't seem in a rush to get back to them. He concluded our talk with, 'Well, I think cyclists are good people!' We shook hands in agreement, and he went to his car and I entered the supermarket. When I came back out, he was still in his car, keeping an eye on my bike.

I was approached by another Norwegian man in the line for the Molde ferry. His hair was white, too. He drove a small, blue Mercedes and had got out to stretch his legs. I again explained where I'd come from and where I was going. I planned on seeing Atlantic Ocean Road tomorrow, I said. He mentioned that it and nearby Trollstigen – a serpentine road with a 10% gradient and 11 hairpins – had both recently been listed by a big paper as two of the ten best roads in the world. He also confirmed that, at the end of Atlantic Ocean Road, there was an underwater tunnel that I wouldn't be allowed to cycle through, so I'd have to turn around and ride back to the start.

As I spoke to the man, I tried to ignore what I assumed might be symptoms of Tourette syndrome. Whenever I finished describing a detail of my journey, he'd inhale sharply, accompanied by a short 'hya' sound, as if someone had just walked over his grave or he'd remembered the bath was still running. The first time he did it, I stopped talking and looked to see whether he was OK, but he showed no indication that anything was out of the ordinary. So I continued, pretending not to hear the sound in case it was a source of embarrassment for him. It was only weeks later, when I spoke to a local woman with the same habit, I realised the sound was not a sign of overflowing personal anguish, but is used by some Norwegians to say 'How interesting!' Seemingly, it's more prevalent among the older generations.

'After, on your way to Trondheim, you'll cross Bergsøya?' he asked. He'd opened a map on his phone and was pointing to a small island in a fjord to the north. On a map of Norwegian tunnels, I'd seen an off-limits icon next to Bergsøya, so was adamant that using the island as a stepping stone wasn't possible; I'd have to head southeast for half a day to get around the fjord. He looked towards the sky, picturing the route in his mind. 'No, this is not true; there are bridges to Bergsøya; you can cycle there. Yes.' I was sceptical, but thanked him for his advice. He wished me good luck and climbed back into his car as the ferry pulled in.

At a campsite in Molde, I sat on some rocks by the shores of Romdalsfjord, looking at maps and relishing some baked beans I'd heated in the kitchen. Steam drifted from the bowl into the evening air. I checked the tunnel map again. Sure enough, the man was right; there was a way around the tunnel near Bergsøya and I could take bridges to get onto and off of the island, thereby crossing the fjord. This knocked 100 kilometres off of my intended route. I also looked at the route I'd taken that day. I'd climbed over 2,000 metres, more than any day since hiking to Trolltunga. To the south of the fjord were the 222 white peaks of the 'Molde panorama'. Gazing at those far-off mountains from the lapping shores seemed symbolic. I felt that maybe I had entered a new world, one comprised less of cliffs and snow and more of rolling hills and scattered islands.

I awoke the next morning to rays of bright light warming my tent; but, as if sensing my stirring, they were gone by the time I crawled out. The grey Sunday began with an hour-long detour around a short tunnel that was out of bounds for cyclists. The road led through silent industrial estates, where expanses of concrete were strewn with piles of planks, rusty trucks and diggers, and bleak warehouses, all abandoned for the weekend. Even the forest that followed seemed drab, its adolescent trees quivering in the cold headwind, their colours dull beneath the oppressive sky. I stared up at the clouds and pleaded with them to leave. It's summer, take a rest, I told them. If not for the whole season, then give me just one day alone with the sun. One hour?

Stoically, the clouds continued to monitor me as I fought my way through manure-scented gusts. If there was a whisper of enthusiasm for cycling inside of me, it was because, for the first time, I was nearing the coast – not some beach at the end of a fjord in the middle of the country, but the actual coast, the western edge of Norway. 'Fine,' I eventually heard. I looked around me, not knowing where the voice had come from. Then I felt a hint of warmth on my face and hands. I glanced up. There were breaches in the clouds. As if seeing the aurora borealis, I gazed adoringly at the little channels of blue in the sky, wishing I could bottle that simple colour and keep it on a shelf forever.

As I reached the end of the Romsdal Peninsula, the road turned right and I cycled parallel to the coast. Looking through birch trees, which lined a string of fields, I caught glimpses of the Atlantic. If I could have sailed west from there, I'd eventually have reached Greenland, narrowly missing the Faroe Islands (to the south) and Iceland (to the north) on my way. The bend in the road meant that the wind I had been fighting for the last few hours was now on my side. Such was its strength that it was hardly necessary to pedal. I looked up so my handlebars were out of sight and imagined I had suddenly learned to fly. I touched down minutes later near the mouth of Kvernesfjord, where I stood by a stretch of grass occupied by a red boat house. Far across the water was Atlantic Ocean Road, leaping between tiny islands of rock. The steep incline of Storseisundet Bridge, the jewel in the road's crown, sparkled in the sun.

I sped along the road to the first bridge, my senses feeling sharper than they had in some time, as if the glimpses of sunlight had ignited my circuitry, as if the effects of a sedative were wearing off. I could smell the salt and seaweed in the air, feel them in my lungs. The atmosphere was thicker, richer. The squawks of spiralling seagulls cut through the sloshing of the water on the rocks. From cracks in the skerries grew grass and wildflowers, trembling in the blustering wind. In places, the plants covered whole islands, forming meadows, where wooden huts and houses perched. Beyond the shimmering grey-blue water of the fjord's mouth, the hills of the mainland formed a dark, undulating outline. The wind pushed me onward, from island to island. Ahead, a string of campervans hummed along the road, the most distant briefly held up to the heavens by Storseisundet Bridge, before disappearing behind it. I watched them all enjoy those few seconds at the summit of Atlantic Ocean Road, until it was my turn to be blown to the top of the curvaceous bridge, where the seagulls' song reached a resonant crescendo as they watched the fishermen below.

Descending the bridge I noticed a break in the traffic barrier on the other side of the road. I checked for campervans, then dashed across to where a steep grass bank led to an area of barren rock that stuck out into the ocean. I scrambled down the bank with my bike, then continued without it onto the rock. Waves rolled in and crashed against it, filling the air with spray.

I could see, further along the road, a busy car park where tourists were craning their necks to get a better view of the bridge whose shadow I was now in, standing on the rock; I might not be able to cover as many miles on my bike as others could in their vehicles, but I could often see much more within those miles.

But those in the car park, unlike cyclists, could use the underwater tunnel at the north end of the 8-kilometre road. For a while, I watched the procession of campervans rise and fall over the bridge – gulls above them, fishermen below – then hauled my bike back up the bank and returned to the mainland.

On the Romsdal Peninsula again, I headed towards Bergsøya, where I planned to find a forest to camp in. Through the wind came a whisper. 'That's enough,' it said. I looked out over Kvernesfjord and saw that dark clouds had reclaimed the sky. A few rays of alchemic light, however, tore through, changing sections of the charcoal water to bronze. There were fields to my right, most empty, but some with families of horses, from whose nostrils steam drifted into the early evening air. After two hours, the concrete towers and taut white cables of the Bergsøya suspension bridge came into sight. A small stone-walled harbour sheltered beside the ramp of the giant bridge. Within it were fishing boats, from which came a stench that had the local gulls in a frenzy. Atop the bridge, I admired the forested hills of the island, and wondered where among them I would sleep.

At the other end of the bridge was a modern bus terminal. Given Bergsøya's population of 200, the terminal seemed inexplicably large, with a spacious waiting room and capacity for a dozen buses. However, there were neither people nor buses, and I ogled the rows of empty seats inside the waiting room, imagining myself soundly asleep upon them, my bike happily leant against an internal wall. But what if a bus rolls in, I thought, full of pristine Norwegians who want to make use of the room until their connecting bus arrives, and I'm there stinking up the place? I'd be too ashamed to sleep.

Continuing onwards along a main road, I kept my eyes peeled for patches of flat land and, when the coast was clear, scampered off the road to investigate any promising areas, only to find the ground waterlogged. After not too long, I came across a track that led into a woodland, laid my bike down and stamped around among the trees until I found a plot that was dry and not too bumpy. A quick recce revealed a house a stone's throw away, though it seemed unlikely I'd be seen or that it would matter if I were. I got set up and spent my first night on a Norwegian island.

The delicate shadows of leaves danced on the bright nylon of my tent in the morning; the sun was out. I packed up quickly, excited to see the colours of the world in bloom.

I wasn't the only one; a handful of elderly locals had already set up their fishing rods by the time I arrived at the blue pontoon bridge on the east side of Bergsøya. A few nodded and smiled as I rode past. Some gazed at the pine-covered islets in the glistening water. Others had their eyes closed, relishing the warmth on their faces.

The bridge led me to an intricate part of the map. First was Aspøya, an 'island' since 1905, when a tiny canal was created, detaching the hitherto peninsula from the mainland. The road then weaved its way between several lakes, each filled with blossoming lilies, along a cucumber-shaped section of land whose width I crossed just in time for the Kanestraum-to-Halsa ferry. The village of Halsa occupies an isthmus between Halsafjord and Skålvikfjord, the latter being where Keiko, the orca from *Free Willy*, first appeared after being released in Iceland in 2002. (Sadly, he never fully adapted to life in the wild and died in nearby Arasvikfjord the following year.)

As I approached the Møre og Romsdal-Trøndelag county line, clouds filled the sky once again and I entered a lazy cartographer's dream; for the next 60 kilometres, there was scarcely a bend in the road as it followed the ruler-like shoreline of Vinjefjord before entering a long, narrow valley. To deal with the monotony, I took frequent breaks on the side of the road, where there was always a gang of flies waiting for me, the type I referred to as 'the medium bastards' – just your run-of-the-mill flies, endlessly curious about what treasures might be found on one's skin and fast enough to indulge this curiosity with only a low risk of being slapped to death.

As a pink haze crept into the sky in the evening, I came across the entrance to a campsite. 'Mountain Camp' was painted on a plank that hung from a wooden frame and swung in the breeze. I rode in on the long gravel driveway, passing dilapidated caravans and static homes. It was quiet; only the crunching of the stones beneath my tyres broke the silence. A maroon house sat in the centre of the grounds; a wooden structure with its own garden, surrounded by a wire fence. With a little trepidation, I leant my bike against the fence, walked up to the house and knocked on the paint-chipped front door.

The door was secured by a chain on the inside, so it only opened a few inches at first – just enough for a large snout to peek through at crotch level. It sniffed and licked the air excitedly, as someone fiddled with the chain. The moment the door opened fully, the giant owner of the snout burst forth.

I knew instantly I'd like whoever had opened the door; only an agreeable person could have such a magnificent dog. It had deep-set blue eyes, thick fur the colour of coffee, cinnamon and snow, and a tongue that wouldn't quit; with his giant paws on my chest, he tried desperately to lick my face, adamant we would be best friends for life.

Supporting the dog's forelegs with my hands and turning my head towards the door, I asked what breed he was. A Finnish Lapphund, said the man, who had a long grey beard and wore a dusty black-and-red plaid shirt. He was old but looked strong and healthy.

I paid the man a small sum and we took a walk around the grounds. Away from the trailer park section were generous expanses of grass sprinkled with buttercups and fringed by ragged trees. There were only a few campers, so I had my pick of spots. You could go here, the man would say, pointing to one indistinguishable patch of grass after another. Or here, or here. I agreed they were all fine options. In the end, I picked somewhere next to a little communal cabin.

With my tent pitched, I strolled over to the shower blocks. A woman stood outside, her face obscured by a black mesh. I said hi and she responded timidly. By the time I came back out, she'd been joined by a male partner, who wore the same type of garment over his face. I said hi again and they replied in unison. In a lonely corner of the grounds, a tent had been set up. Beside it were two bikes.

I retrieved my plastic bag of battered food from my tent and made for the communal cabin, where I planned to spend some time determining the next stages of my ride. The cabin was musty but cosy, with an electric heater and colourful old cushions scattered across wooden benches. I opened a map, then slapped together some bread and cheese to eat as I scrutinised the upcoming roads. As I took a greedy bite, the door swung open. It was the couple from outside the shower blocks. Their faces were still hidden. I said hi once more and again they responded in sync. We stared at each other in silence for several long seconds, until they finally raised their hands to remove their headwear.

'Those *damn* knotts!' howled the man. He shook his head and grinned at me. He ran a slender hand through his short auburn hair, as if to comb out any insects.

'The what?' I asked. 'Oh, you mean the little bastards?' I'd been ravaged by them while setting up my tent.

'What?' he returned.

'The little bastards. You know, the blackflies.'

'Exactly,' he said. 'Those damn blackflies!'

He strolled over and stuck out his hand. 'I'm Marco,' he said, then pointed to his girlfriend. 'And this is Ida.'

Her headwear had been concealing long fair hair and sky-blue eyes.

'Hi,' she said, with a disarming smile.

They each took a seat. Ida placed a bag on the table, then retrieved from it some bread and sliced meat.

'You're a cyclist, too?' asked Marco, pointing in the direction of my tent and bike. 'Are you headed to or from the North Cape?'

'Towards it, but only as far Tromsø.'

The couple were Oslovians, had come from the North Cape and were headed for Kristiansand on the southern edge of the country.

'You'll be joining the 17 soon, I suppose? We just left it a couple of days ago,' said Marco.

'The 17?'

'Yeah, the FV17. The Coastal Highway.'

Seeing I didn't know about the 17, they stared at me in disbelief. If not the 17, they asked, how would I get to Tromsø?

I pointed to a large road on my map, the E6, a 3,000-kilometre route starting in the south of Sweden, entering Norway near Oslo, and finishing near the Norwegian-Russian border, just north of Finland.

Marco nodded. 'Yeah, you *could* do that – if you have a thing for traffic, or something.'

'And if you don't like the ocean,' added Ida.

They smiled at each other.

The 17, they told me, started about 200 kilometres away near Steinkjer, a substantial town on the northern shores of Trondheimsfjord. From there, it made its way to the coast – the proper coast – where it wound along the jagged edge of the country. After 630 kilometres, it ended near Bodø, the town from which I planned to take a ferry to the Lofoten Islands. Fondly,

Marco and Ida traced their fingers along the road on my map, recalling times they'd escaped bad weather by jumping on one of the many ferries and nights they'd camped by the sea with no one else around.

As well as the 17, they recommended places that lay beyond it. If I was headed to Lofoten, they said, I should check out Andøya, an island on the adjoining Vesterålen archipelago. 'It's completely unreal,' said Ida, 'the colour of the water. Like you're in the Caribbean.' From Andøya I could take a ferry to the island of Senja, the home of Segla, a fjord-side mountain shaped like an alien fortress.

When they'd finished eating, they wished me good luck, then redonned their black headwear. 'I'm ready for ya, ya little bastards!' roared Marco before opening the cabin door.

Shortly after they left, I retreated to my tent, where I dreamt of crystal waters lapping at the dark feet of otherworldly mountains.

Mist crept across the campsite in the morning. The owner was strolling the grounds wearing jeans and boots and the same black-and-red plaid shirt as the day before. His Finnish Lapphund proudly strutted by his side. I waved goodbye to them as I rolled back down the gravel to the road, then turned in the direction of Trondheim. From a terminal a little outside the city, I hoped to later take a ferry to the western shores of Trondheimsfjord.

Since I was several hundred metres above sea level and headed to the fjord, the route was downhill. As I descended, moist air saturated my clothes and skin. My bike, too, was enveloped by the damp, rendering my already ineffective brakes just about useless, a problem compounded by the buckle that had emerged in my four-day-old rear wheel. I thought back to the bike shop in Stryn and the uneasy look on the young mechanic's face as I thanked him. Not a minute after I'd concluded that the wheel should hold out if I were careful, several spokes snapped. A roar came from below as the tyre rubbed against the frame. Instinctively, I pulled on my brakes, though of course the rear did nothing, and the front was impotent against the weight of myself and my bags, the descent and the lubricious air. With the tips of my shoes I could just about reach the road, so I pressed down as hard as I could and eventually came to a halt.

As the beating of my heart subsided, I was struck by the absence of sound. No wind, no people, no traffic, just weatherworn trees and desolate fields. It would take hours to reach the nearest town on foot. But there was nothing I could do besides trudge forth.

I watched the white painted lines creep beneath me. I studied the tiny stones that comprised the surface of the road and the countless weeds in the earth beside me. They were normally a blur, though now all had distinct forms. I wondered whether these details disappeared when there were no eyes upon them, whether reality took measures to not overburden itself. No, the paint and the stones and the weeds were always there, and would still be there long after I had finished my trip and had returned home, where I'd think about them from time to time, existing unseen and in silence.

Not wanting to acknowledge the unmoving horizon, I looked up infrequently. Just in case anything of use had entered my world while I'd been staring at the ground. An hour into my march, I raised my eyes and was stopped dead by a sign beside the road. It pointed towards a birch-lined driveway, at the end of which were several large houses. Painted on the sign was *sykkel*, one of the few Norwegian words I'd learned. In the middle of all of this nothingness, there might just be the one thing I need: a bike mechanic.

The grey stones of the driveway led to a large workshop, its panels painted a proud burgundy. Asleep on a deck at the workshop's entrance was an old Alsatian. Hearing my footsteps, he opened his eyes and lazily wagged his tail. A ginger cat with light green irises tiptoed across the deck, sniffing the potted plants. All was in order, they concluded.

As I began to make pessimistic assumptions about the significance of the padlock on the workshop door, I heard footsteps behind me.

'New wheel, is it?' came a man's voice.

I turned to see a svelte 50-year-old in blue overalls wiping his hands on a rag. He strode towards me with manic eyes.

'It'll have to be,' he said, gripping the wheel and giving it a shake. 'There's no fixing this. It would just break again. Where'd you get this? It's from a kid's bike.'

Before I could respond, he removed the padlock and disappeared into the workshop.

He returned several minutes later with a wheel. 'This'll work,' he said, patting the rim. 'No way it's gonna break, either.' He pointed to a sticker with a number written on it. 'This is the price. It's OK?' I converted the kroner into pounds in my mind. The wheel cost a third of what I'd paid for my entire bike. (Sure, my bike was a piece of crap, but still.) I looked around to confirm I was in the middle of nowhere; there was no chance of a finding second mechanic with whom the first might compete on price.

'Sounds good!' I said, then stifled a cry as the man vanished into the workshop again, this time with my bike.

I took a seat on the decking and consoled myself by stroking the animals.

Every few minutes, the man would reappear to tell me he had noticed something that was on the verge of disintegration: the chain, the brake pads and cables, the front tyre. 'Shall I fix it?' he'd ask. 'I guess you better had,' I'd say, not daring to ask the cost, then would stare into the sad, uncomprehending eyes of the Alsatian.

'Listen to me,' said the man as he eventually wheeled my bike back out of the workshop. 'You must never take this touring again. It's made for going to the supermarket, nothing more. It's very bad. The whole bike, it's... it's very bad.'

I promised him I would heed his advice, though knew I'd probably end up riding my cheap ol' bike until it split in two or until I'd saved up enough pocket money to replace it.

I paid up, the beep of the credit card machine coinciding with a sinking in my heart, then plodded back up the driveway.

But the pain of the expense dissipated as soon as I was back on the road. I couldn't remember a time when my bike had felt so good. When I pulled the brakes, I stopped; when I shifted gears, they shifted. Previously, my bike had made a game of surprising me with gear changes; I'd request a different gear, but it wouldn't come until some unforeseen time in the future, at which point the abrupt change in resistance would cause me to slip from my pedals. Gone too was the bumping from the buckled wheel; the new wheel rolled as if in the vacuum of space. Clearly, the snapping of my spokes had been divine intervention and I was indebted to Odin.

I became so engrossed in riding, so connected to the sleek machine beneath me, that I became oblivious of time. After coasting to a stop in the bleak ferry terminal near Trondheim, I checked my progress. I couldn't believe I had covered 75 kilometres since leaving the campsite; it was as if someone else had been riding all morning and I had just switched places with them at the terminal and was taking credit.

When the ferry arrived, I strode on, found a comfortable window-side seat and surveyed Trondheimsfjord, hoping to spot one of the giant squids for which it's famed.

Life continued to feel effortless on the other side. I tore along the coast, admiring luxurious houses nestled within the forested hills overlooking the fjord. Several hours later, I arrived at a quiet campsite and chatted with a middle-aged Dutch couple in the reception. They were cycling to the North Cape from Amsterdam. Having met Marco and Ida the previous evening, I had the impression that I had now drifted into the cycle-touring veins of the country. I paid the owner a very reasonable 50 kroner (US$5), then explored the grounds. The campsite had its own beach, equipped with rustic barbecues, and a pier. I spent the evening plodding along the stony beach, wondering where the driftwood had come from and how it had found its way there. Above the water, a blush infused the sky. I held the colour in my mind as I retreated to my tent and slid into sleep.

I saw the Dutch couple again the following afternoon. I was sitting at the side of the road with my back against a pile of logs, chewing some stale bread and swiping at flies. They nodded as they crawled past, too out of breath to talk; we were in the hills a little southeast of Steinkjer. A while later, I stood, swung my backpack over my shoulders and set off in pursuit, having decided to make a game of catching them. As I began to suspect I'd lost them, they appeared in the distance, the mirrors on their handlebars flickering in a brief moment of sunlight. We were approaching a long, steep descent, which would take us back to the fjord. I changed into my highest gear, leaned forward and pedalled harder. The wind roaring in my ears, I whooshed past the woman. Her husband, however, seeing me in his mirror, upped his pace. A scene from *Moonraker* entered my mind where Bond, freefalling from a plane, is chased through the sky by a steel-teethed henchman. To reduce drag, I held my elbows by my side and pointed my knees dead ahead. Inch by inch, I gained on the man until eventually I overtook him, imagining, optimistically, that we looked like a pair of falcons.

I knew I'd been in the countryside too long as I rolled into Steinkjer; the town of 12,000 seemed like a sprawling metropolis, what with its train tracks, two-lane highways and bustling restaurants. But as quickly as the scents and sounds of urban life appeared, they vanished and the road was once again flanked by forests and fields as far as the eye could see. The dimming of the eternal light began as I passed through Asp, a hamlet comprised of a dozen houses, a petrol station and a concrete-heavy Toyota dealership. The significance of Asp lies only its location; it marks the beginning of the 17. I smiled as I turned onto it, knowing Marco and Ida had been in the exact spot a couple of days earlier, headed the other way. It felt like the beginning of where I was supposed to be.

As I passed a road sign listing the names of distant towns, a van careened past with its hazard lights on, then came to a sharp stop. I couldn't imagine what the driver might want with me, but there was nobody else around, so had to conclude I was the reason they had pulled over. Had I dropped something? Had my rear light stopped working again? Had I insulted someone's mother?

A tall man jumped out and slid open the side door. 'Don't go anywhere!' he shouted as I approached. He climbed into the rear of the van, where he began rummaging around. Obediently, I pulled my brakes and waited beside the flashing amber lights.

To my relief, he was smiling when he climbed back out. He strode towards me with a bulging plastic bag. 'Here,' he said, holding out the bag, 'I have something for you!'

I took it and peered inside.

'It's lefse,' he explained, 'a traditional Norwegian flatbread, made from potatoes. I think you must eat a lot if you're cycling all day?'

I grinned and confirmed that it was true, then imagined the succulent bread filled with banana and peanut butter. It was only bread, but I couldn't help but be moved by the gesture, and I feared my eyes might begin to shimmer as we stood beside the van's blinking lights.

'Thank you,' I said.

'Not at all,' he replied, as a stream of cars swerved around us. 'Well, I better get out of the road and let you be on your way. Where is it you're going, anyhow?'

'Tromsø.'

'Wow, Tromsø, it's a long way!'

'Seems to be,' I said.

We shook hands, then he hopped back in his van and I squeezed the bag of bread into a pannier.

I trundled along the road until I came across a small pine forest, where I set up my tent and let the hoots of birds and the cries of reindeer sing me to sleep.

In the silence of the morning I lay thinking about my ride so far. There had been moments of masochistic satisfaction, such as when dragging my bike to Trolltunga, and there were frequent moments of awe, such as when the fleetingness of life was magnified by the immortal mountains and fjords. But when the days grew long there was often boredom, too. Times when I could no longer keep the grey skies out of my soul, when they would seep in and perfuse me with apathy.

To address this, I had tried to find things to see on the way, but my desire to cover ground always trumped my curiosity about what I might find inside that little folk museum or in that local artist's studio. I decided, then, to take a different approach to tackling my boredom. I would ride harder.

As I wheeled my bike back through the forest to the road, I visualised how I would ride henceforth. My heart must always be thumping; my legs must always be spinning; my lungs always heaving. If it was another grey, drizzly day, then good. That would help me focus. All that existed today were my heart, legs and lungs.

I checked the time as I set off; I wouldn't even think of stopping, not even momentarily, until I'd ridden for an hour. Once the hour was up, I'd shove food into my mouth, wash it down with water, then do another hour; I'd repeat this cycle indefinitely.

Whenever doubts about my stamina entered my mind, I forced myself to examine the symptoms. *My heart rate is elevated*, I'd report to myself; another part of me would say, *yes, but it's not going to explode*. Likewise, *My legs are burning* was countered with, *yes, but they're not going to catch on fire*. I wanted to view types of pain objectively, much as I might see a tree or the colour blue and apply the labels *tree* or *blue* to them; they were a part of my experience, but had no control over me. I also asked myself, *are you at your physical limit?* Of course, the answer was always no. *Then go faster.*

I coasted into a campsite in mid afternoon and checked how far I'd ridden: 110 kilometres, a distance I considered respectable for a full day. The reception was closed, but the prices were written on a board. It was expensive and since, for the first time, there seemed to be lots of wild camping spots, I continued onwards.

With 140 kilometres covered, a crack of thunder tore open the ash-coloured sky, unleashing a torrent of frigid water. I took it as a sign to stop. Beside me, on the other side of a traffic barrier, was a steep bank. It was thick with pine trees, but between them I had caught glimpses of a lake. If

I could somehow get to its shores, I thought, there might be somewhere to camp. It was also possible there would be nowhere but it was worth a shot, if only to shelter in the forest. So I hauled my bike over the traffic barrier and took my first cautious steps on the wet earth of the bank. Once out of sight of the road, I laid my bike down and continued the descent without it, holding onto branches to prevent myself from sliding through the mud. After a while, the ground flattened and I forged a path around fallen trees until I came to a clearing by the rippled water. This would do.

The rain eased as I headed back into the woods to retrieve my bike, and had stopped by the time I made it back to the grassy clearing. I was surprised to see that the rocks by the edge of the water were strewn with mollusc shells and seaweed; what I had thought was a lake – I was a long way from the western edge of the country – was actually a very long and narrow fjord. I then noticed that the seaweed wasn't just on the waterside rocks but also scattered across the grass I planned to camp on. I picked some up. It was brittle. I hoped this meant it had been blown up onto the grass by the wind and had not been taken there by a recent high tide.

I pitched on a flattish and not overly soaked spot. Inside my tent, I listened to the water lapping at the shore, keeping the entrance unzipped so I could admire where I was and relish having this spot all to myself. A reward for a good day on the road, a day in which I had been so fixated on riding that there had been no room for boredom.

Tall cliffs dominated the far side of the fjord. There was a single wooden cabin beneath them where I could just make out a man loading a small boat. Later, he untied the ropes that secured the boat to his jetty, then set off in the direction of the ocean. A faint hum came from his outboard engine. Already tiny beneath the cliffs, I watched him grow ever smaller, until he finally disappeared and I fell asleep.

D J ROBINSON

Møre og Romsdal and Trøndelag Statistics

- Distance (trip total): 662 kilometres (1,318 kilometres)

- Climbing (trip total): 8,194 metres (18,061 metres)

- Highest point: 561 metres (Ørskogfjellet Skisenter)

- Island Rides project distance: 3,802 kilometres

- Island Rides project climbing: 37,944 metres

Nordland

Aye, aye! and I'll chase him round Good Hope, and round the Horn, and round the Norway Maelstrom[4], and round perdition's flames before I give him up. And this is what ye have shipped for, men! To chase that white whale on both sides of land, and over all sides of earth, till he spouts black blood and rolls fin out. What say ye, men, will ye splice hands on it, now? I think ye do look brave.

Captain Ahab in *Moby Dick* by Herman Melville

Through the morning mist that blanketed the fjord, I could see the boat again. From wherever the man had gone, he had returned and was now, I guessed, asleep in his cabin or preparing breakfast. Scarcely awake, my thoughts were still dreamlike. I pictured myself standing on the shell-covered rocks, waving both arms and calling out to the man. He'd emerge from his cabin and I'd start jumping, feigning an emergency. He'd leap in his boat, then speed towards me, before scraping to a halt on the rocks. 'What is it?' he'd ask, looking alarmed. 'What do you need?' And I'd respond, 'You don't have any coffee, do you?'

He'd at first be annoyed about being lured across the fjord for this, but would soon see the funny side. He'd smile and, without a word, would reach down into the boat for a thermos flask. (How it got there, I don't know.) He'd toss it ashore and I'd catch it. With great pleasure, I'd fill a cup with the steaming elixir.

I smiled at the thought of the warm cup between my hands and of the coffee banishing the cold from my bones. I knew this was not likely to happen, but also knew that a half dozen ferries connected the upcoming fragments of the 17 and there was always coffee on ferries. Only once had there not been and my caffeine levels became so dangerously low that, from the comfort of a warm lounge, I mistook the sounds of docking for those of a mysterious mechanical problem and ended up completing the hour-long crossing twice.

It was great.

I liked the ferries a lot. They were frequent, so I rarely checked departure times before arriving at the terminal; I'd just roll in past the queue of cars, join any other cyclists and pedestrians by the ramp, then await the guy or gal selling tickets. When the ferry arrived, I'd find a wall to lean my bike against, then head inside to drool over the offerings in the café. As well as coffee, the ferries often had hot food – waffles served with jam, *lefse* with butter and cinnamon, or toast with *brunost*, a brown Norwegian cheese that tastes like caramel. Loaded with a tray of the above, I'd find a seat by a window and/or radiator, then stare at the water in a sugar-induced euphoria.

Most ferries run about every hour between early morning and mid evening, except in remote locations or when the crossing is long. For example, the ferry from Andenes, at the northern tip of the Vesterålen archipelago, to Senja takes close to two hours and only runs two or three times per day, depending on the time of year. Norwegian ferries are operated by various companies, so the easiest way for me to look up times was to Google them or to use a transport-specific search engine, like Rome2rio. At the terminal, departure times are usually listed on a staff cabin beside the ramp.

Besides being well stocked and warm, the ferries are relatively cheap. I typically paid between 40 and 80 kroner (US$4–8). Of course, more substantial crossings are more expensive. For the three-hour ferry ride from Bodø to Moskenes (Lofoten), for instance, I paid about 220 kroner (US$21). I took this particular ferry at 03.15 in the morning and the price seemed very reasonable for several hours of sleep on a cushioned bench, which felt like the height of luxury after weeks in a damp tent.

As mentioned earlier, the Norwegian government would like to do away with many of the ferries. The 1,300-kilometre E39, which I spent some time on between Atlantic Ocean Road and Trondheim, includes nine ferries, the most of any road in Europe, and there are plans to get rid of them all. Replacing ferries with tunnels or bridges would reduce travel times and help smaller towns to maintain their populations as there would be less reason to relocate for work. However, since many fjords are several hundred metres deep and several kilometres wide, tunnels are often not an option as they would be too steep and the technology to build the bridges is still being developed. Essentially, they will need to float, but do so without preventing large ships from passing beneath.

The estimate of US$40 billion is one reason replacing the ferries is controversial. But it's more than the cost. The ferries are part of the charm of Norway. They're a reason for people to take a break from driving, to stretch their legs, to have coffee or waffles with friends and family, to talk to one another. For cyclists, they're a chance to get out of the rain, to escape the discomfort of the saddle, to meet other adventurers. Undoubtedly, time would be saved by replacing the ferries, but moments would be lost.

The mollusc shells and seaweed crunched beneath my feet as I left the clearing and headed into the forest. I retraced my path around the fallen trees, then headed back up the long, slippery bank, taking my bags up before returning for my bike. When I reached the road and set off, I could feel the light rain that I had only heard in the forest. Gaps in the trees revealed the hazy water of the fjord, wherein islands of pine floated like wandering ghost ships. I crossed the fjord via a lonely, single-lane, suspension bridge, then disappeared into a dark tunnel. On the other side was Foldereid, the last village before Nordland, its edge marked by a white, wooden church. I made a beeline across a large car park to the entrance of a supermarket. There was a bike outside.

I spotted Hugo as I was bagging my items. He was sitting by himself in a café adjoining the supermarket, waiting for me to turn in his direction. When I did, he smiled and waved. I bought a coffee and went to say hi.

"Ow was your night by the fjord?' he asked, the question's leading *h* swallowed by his French accent, like the one in his name.

I gave him a look. *How do you know where I slept?* He grinned, then explained that a cycling couple had mentioned seeing a lone cyclist and there weren't many around. He'd spoken to the couple at the campsite I'd briefly considered staying at. 'There weren't too many places to camp after there. The best place was by the fjord, so I guess that's where you stayed.'

I recalled the couple. Even though we hadn't met, I somehow felt connected to them, as if we were part of the same club, in which information travelled not through fingers and satellites, but through mouths and roads. The 17 was a cable.

'I don't usually eat like this,' said Hugo, looking down at the table and scratching his long, chestnut hair through his beanie. He was enjoying a feast of beer, peanuts, avocado, bread and chocolate cake. 'But today's my birthday. I'm twenty-four.' He slid the cake in my direction and asked me to help him finish it.

I spent a pleasant hour there, gallantly assisting Hugo with his cake and learning about his life in the south of France, where he'd spent the last three years working as a civil engineer. He'd been terribly bored, he told me, so one day packed his bags, got on his bike and headed north. He was on his way to the North Cape. It was touching to see how happy he now seemed. His face was often lit with a boyish smile as he sipped his beer and looked through the window at the bleak weather, as if he had envisioned this very moment long before.

I would have liked to have spent more time with him, to maybe ride together for a while, but it was only yesterday I had resolved to push harder, and clearly Hugo's plans for his birthday didn't include gritting his teeth and doing battle with the wind and rain.

'I just have to buy something else before I go,' I said. 'I'll be back in a minute.' When I returned, I handed him a can of beer. 'Happy birthday!' Organising my things, I asked, 'Where will you go after the North Cape?'

'This I don't know,' he said. 'Not for sure, anyway. Probably south through Finland, the Baltics and Poland. Then maybe Asia. Who knows.'

We shook hands and wished each other good luck. Had I thought to, I would have taken his details. I wonder where he is now.

Filled with coffee and birthday cake, I welcomed the rain. It suited this part of the country, I decided, fit it like a musty old jacket. It was only right that somewhere so remote should be shrouded in mist, as if I were cycling along the border of reality. I sang to myself as I watched the clouds caress the cliffs. *Life is old there, older than the trees. Younger than the mountains, growing like a breeze.*

The wind howled as I neared the Atlantic, and on the shore a young woman in fluorescent waterproofs was being battered by the elements as she sold tickets for the Holm-to-Vennesund ferry. The boat swung from side to side as it chugged among the white manes of the waves, then it bounced along the car tyres that hung from the wall on the other side. As if I were being banished from this obscure part of the world, the wind shoved me north, and I sped along at 25 kph without pedalling and at 40 kph if I did.

Soaked, I arrived at a bizarre campsite on an empty section of road. Scattered throughout the grounds were crudely carved statues of people in traditional Norwegian clothing – women in long, thick dresses, men in wide-brimmed hats and waistcoats – their bulging eyes peering through the evening fog. They were oddly proportioned; some had long legs and short torsos, others stubby arms and gargantuan heads; all had bulbous noses and suspiciously innocent expressions. They were engaged in old-timey pursuits, building barns or riding horse-drawn carts. In addition, there were several ploughs, a stone well and cutesy red-and-white cabins adorned with antlers. There were porcelain sheep and wolves and children's toys – a red tricycle, a rain-soaked slide, a rusty swing.

Feeling like the cop in *The Wicker Man*, I opened a creaking door and ventured into the tiny reception area. It was empty. I called out into a hallway. After a while, an elderly woman appeared. Tall and broad, she probably knew her way around a barn raising. She was the only Norwegian I encountered who spoke virtually no English.

'*Kabin?*' she asked. (Fortunately, even I could translate this.)

I had planned on sleeping in my tent, though it was still wet from pitching on soggy ground the night before, so I asked how much a cabin would be.

The woman held up six fingers, which I took to mean 600 kroner (US$57).

As I was accustomed to paying very little or nothing for accommodation, this seemed a large sum, but now the idea of not spending the night in my tent had entered my mind, there was no fighting it. It took control of my body and, despite the protests of my internal accountant, I handed my card to the woman.

'*Nei,*' she said, looking over her shoulder, as if checking for the tax man. She rubbed her thumb and index finger together. *Cash only.*

Surprised – everyone in Norway had accepted card payments, even ramshackle establishments miles from anywhere – I looked inside my wallet. It was clear from a glance I didn't have the cash, but I counted it anyway.

'I don't have it,' I said.

The woman beckoned me closer with a finger, then counted the money in my wallet herself, checking that I wasn't hiding any. She pulled out 350, looked over her shoulder once more, then said OK.

'Really?' I asked. 'It's OK?'

She nodded and reached for a key. 'Yes, no problem.'

As she handed me the key, she glared at a pool of water that had formed at my feet. I asked, pinching my wet clothes, if there was somewhere I could do laundry. '*Nei*,' she said, with a shake of her head, then mimicked putting clothes on a line, repeating *kabin* each time she hung an imaginary item.

Like the grounds, the inside of the little cabin was bedecked with decorations – bowls of pine cones, artificial flowers, tiny landscape paintings, hanging plates. The cupboards and drawers were filled with enough crockery and cutlery, each piece unique, to serve a barracks. There were cushioned benches, a child-sized bunk bed and thick, colourful curtains. Most importantly, there was a radiator.

I turned this on as soon as I saw it, then removed my jacket and draped it over a nearby chair. But most of my other clothes were wet too, as was my tent; to have everything dry by the morning, to justify the expense of the cabin, I would need another heat source. Looking around, I spotted an electric hob, and turned both burners up to 10, then removed more items of clothing and identified places to hang them – the frame of the bunk bed, more chairs, curtain rails, tea towel hooks.

With vapour flowing from the hanging items, I changed into my remaining dry clothes, then stood over the hob, absorbing its heat. The air was hot and thick in my nose and lungs, the way it feels in a sauna. Through the window, the rain hammered down. I imagined myself out there on the grass, setting up my tent, climbing inside, and creating a pile of wet clothes beside my punctured air mattress. I saw myself shivering and staring at the nylon. With the heat from the hob beginning to release the tension from my muscles, I was grateful to have avoided that version of reality.

I awoke to silence; the rain had stopped.

I opened my cabin door to peer at the sky. It was filled with light grey clouds. Benevolent clouds, I concluded; not the type to urinate on the masses. Checking the weather report, I saw that the meteorologists had reached the same conclusion (though had used different wording).

I heard a faint crunching sound. A rugged woman with short grey hair sauntered about on the gravel between the cabins and the showers, smoking. She looked up at the sky between inhalations, blowing plumes towards the heavens.

'North or south?' she asked when she saw me standing in the doorway next to my bike. She had a thick French accent.

'North,' I said.

She nodded. 'Me too, me too. But I'm staying 'ere another day, until the weather improves. I'm done with riding in the rain. Done, I tell you.'

I told her the forecast was good.

'No. No, it's not,' she said. 'It will rain. Yes, it will. I can promise you that.'

'Really? Damn. I think I'll have to risk it. I need to keep moving.'

'Your life,' she said.

I stepped back into my cabin and began retrieving my clothes from the various hooks and edges I'd hung them on. The woman was still outside when I left, wrapped in a jacket and slumped back on a chair outside her cabin, still smoking and looking at the sky.

I waved as I left and she gave me a look that said *it's your life; you're free to make whatever decisions you want, even if they're terrible.*

The clouds began to clear shortly afterwards. I pictured the woman in her chair, jolted by the sight of blue creeping into the sky. *Merde*, she'd think. *The Englishman was right. The bloody Englishman was right!*

Although only brief, my interaction with the woman added to the sense that I was part of something – a tradition of cycling the old Coastal Highway. I felt connected not only to those I shared the road with, but also to the thousands who had ridden it before and to those who would in the future. We were like a chain stretching through time. After leaving the campsite, I passed an elderly man on a touring bike whose wide smile and jubilant wave suggested he felt something similar. A moment later, I spotted a cycling-inspired piece of art: someone had dressed a mannequin in waterproofs, drawn a smile on her face, and placed her on a bike that spanned a small stream. There was a paddle wheel in the stream and a chain connecting it to the bike so the pedals span and the mannequin appeared to be cycling. It was a little creepy, but confirmed I was now in the heart of cycling country.

With glimpses of clear sky and ocean views, I eased up on the 'speed or death' mentality of the previous two days; I was happy just to cruise along. The roads, flanked by a meadow-lined coast on one side and mountains on the other, were often only accessible by ferry; traffic from the ferries would pass me in short bursts, before leaving me alone again with the quiet of nature. In the fields, lambs and calves clumsily plodded under the watchful eyes of their parents. Beside the ferry terminals, fishing boats slept in stone-walled harbours. Above, seagulls grouped together to see off large birds of prey.

By the time I reached Leirfjord, the sun had started its partial descent, and it was time to look for somewhere to sleep. I crossed the golden waters of the fjord via Helgeland Bridge, which, with its diamond-shaped towers and array of diagonal cables, seemed like a stringed instrument of the gods. Feeling minuscule upon it, I stopped to look west, where the edge of Norway disintegrates into a thousand fragments. On the larger islands, the mountains leant north, as if their summits were drawn to the Pole.

The fjord behind me, I rode through a landscape of farmhouses, fields and forests, searching for somewhere flat and out of sight. I careened off the road at one point to inspect one promising-looking area, only to have my bike sink to its hubs in bog. After drenching my rarely dry shoes and socks to pull myself out, I continued along the road. As it approached midnight, I came across an overgrown track by a small, heather-covered hill. I nudged my bike to the top, then prodded the soggy earth with my feet. Knowing I wouldn't find anywhere drier, I pitched my tent, racing from corner to corner with my pegs to outrun the little bastard welcoming party.

For the next two days I followed the coast, where jagged islands burst through placid waters and occasional villages clung to the shores – scatterings of wooden huts and houses, always painted red and white. For the most part, I had the road to myself. I passed one other cyclist, who had ridden from Hamburg, and asked him whether he was enjoying his trip. 'Sometimes yes, sometimes no,' was his response, which was hard to argue with (and very German). The ocean only escaped my adoring gaze when I rode through tunnels, which were so cold I could feel the change in temperature a while before entering them; the cold was due to more than the mere absence of sunlight, as if they bore through ancient glaciers. I was, after all, approaching the Arctic Circle.

I eventually crossed the line one morning on a ferry from Kilboghavn to Jektvik. An announcement over the speakers said that on the shore was a monument marking the spot. Sitting by the window, I was encircled by camera-wielding tourists when the announcement was made. Already very happy to be on a ferry, drinking coffee and eating hot chips, I joined them in staring in wonder at the monument. It was the first day of July and there was not a cube of ice or a flake of snow in sight. Not a single polar bear either. It wasn't how I'd pictured the Arctic, but man, it was the *Arctic* nonetheless. And I had cycled there.

The only change on the north side of the line was that it was wetter. Dark clouds shed their ballast on the trees, rocks and road. Water fell silently in thin white lines on the faces of distant cliffs across the fjords; it formed new rivers through the roadside forests; it covered the road and sloshed beneath my tyres; it drummed on the polyester of my jacket. The clouds also brought a gloom that dulled the colours of the landscapes. When I stopped beside a fjord for something to eat, I stared at the bright orange nectarine I'd brought that morning in Jektvik, as if I'd discovered something from an alien world, where there was warmth and sunlight and an ease about life.

I was snapped out of my reverie by a car horn. A man in a brown people carrier held his arm out through the open window. Something was in his hand. 'I think this is yours, no?' A wallet.

I was struck by that terror you get when you think you've lost something, when you stop whatever you're doing and start madly patting your pockets. I rushed over and took the wallet. But when I opened it, something wasn't quite right. I examined the ID card. *No. That's not me.*

Still, I was hesitant to give the wallet back. *What if I'm delirious and no longer recognise myself? That does look a little like me.*

The man started to look at me suspiciously, then reached for the wallet. 'I don't think it's yours, is it?' I gave a small shake of my head. No. I slowly returned the wallet to within his grasp. He took it, then wound up his window and drove off, his tyres flinging water into the air. I opened the little bag strapped to my top tube and stem, relieved to see my wallet sleeping soundly inside.

I met the owner of the lost wallet an hour later. Arnaud was standing by the ramp at the Ågskardet ferry terminal, reading a science fiction novel.

'Did you get it back?' I asked, coasting to a stop next to his pristine, navy blue bike.

'Pardon me?'

'Your wallet.'

'Ah, yes! My wallet! I did! 'Ow do you know about that?'

I told him about the man in the people carrier and how I had thought the person on the ID looked like me. Arnaud, from French-speaking Geneva, was tall and slim and, like me, had dark hair and eyes.

We would discover on the short ferry ride to Forøy that we were both nerds too. While I had trained in neuroscience, Arnaud had dedicated himself to maths. For his most recent job at a science museum in Paris, he had designed a bike with non-circular wheels. Lots of shapes have a constant width when rotated, he explained; any polygon with an odd number of sides, in fact. Therefore, with a little trickery, they can be used to make a bike that will actually ride very smoothly. I asked him why he hadn't, then, brought this special bike to Norway. He laughed and explained that, although comfortable, his bike was not at all 'efficient' (his favourite word).

'Shall we ride together a while?' I asked as we alighted the ferry. 'Since we're doppelgängers and all.'

'Yes, let's do it,' he said.

Arnaud had started riding in Trondheim and, like me, was headed for Lofoten, where he would stay on a friend's farm.

'*Non*, we 'ave to go this way,' he said as we reached the road. 'We must say goodbye to our friend the 17 for a while.' He pointed to his map. There was a long tunnel we weren't allowed through. Perfectly straight, it was known among locals as the place to test your car's top speed. I had been on the same road for five days and had become complacent about checking my route. Assuming I wouldn't have been brazen enough to go through the tunnel, Arnaud saved me from what would have been a 50-kilometre ride to its entrance and back.

As we set off down a smaller road, we passed road signs that warned motorists of reindeer. I told Arnaud I must have seen a hundred of these signs, but not a single reindeer. The closest I'd got was hearing them as I drifted off in a forest a few days earlier. I had, however, seen a growling badger, a shy fox, a sheep on the roof of a farm and a shit-ton of flies. I'd also been chased along the road by a pair of seagulls. Arnaud had seen loads of reindeer, he said, as if it was getting boring. To my amazement, one sauntered into the road not a minute later. It paused for a moment as if allowing us a proper look and we stopped to admire him – his smoke-grey and snow-white coat, his onyx eyes, his immense antlers. When the hum of a distant car broke the silence, he trotted off into the safety of the trees. Only when he'd been completely consumed by the forest did I start riding again. 'Well, there you are,' said Arnaud, 'now you 'ave seen one.'

Arnaud told me about his life as we rode side by side along the empty coastal road towards another ferry terminal. Before the science museum, he'd spent a year studying in Copenhagen, where he lived on less than €500 per month. After finding a small, ground-floor apartment, he invited as many people as he could to move in and then began sleeping in the conservatory. For food, he raided bins outside shops and visited markets at the end of each day to ask merchants for anything they hadn't been able to sell. He'd then go to a community centre, where he'd pool his loot with whatever else others had gathered, and they'd spend the evening cooking and eating together. After Norway, he planned to take up a teaching position in Geneva and live in an old building with a communal living area. Judging by his clothes and the way he spoke, he was not from a poor family. His frugality seemed to be self-imposed, an expression of environmental conscientiousness, perhaps, or a rejection of the luxury for which his home city is famed.

'I'm trying to think of an English word,' he said as we disembarked the Vassdalsvik-to-Ørnes ferry and re-joined the 17, where rain awaited us. 'Is it bran teezar?' he asked. I frowned at the wet and now-busy road, trying to guess what he meant. 'You know, like a reedal.'

'Oh, you mean brain teaser?'

'Yes, that's what I said – bran teezar. You like them?'

'Sure,' I said, getting onto my bike.

'*Bon.* There is more traffic 'ere, so maybe it is a good time to think instead of talk.'

I nodded.

'OK, 'ere is the first one…[5] He explained the problem as we stood in the rain, then we set off towards a local supermarket, where I bought a six pack of Tuborg, a Danish beer that reminded Arnaud of Copenhagen. As the girl at the till scanned our items, I told him I had a solution to the problem, which required finding the heaviest of nine identical-looking objects by using a balance scale only twice. I outlined my answer as I paid.

'*C'est bon*,' he said, nodding in approval. 'So, ready for another?'

'Sure,' I said again, pulling the drawstring of my jacket hood and stepping back out into the rain.

This one involved three people standing in a line, wearing either black or white hats, who had to determine the colour of their own hat. Only one of them figures out the colour of their hat, but what is it and how do they know?

I stared at the spray from Arnaud's rear wheel as we set off along the coast once more, picturing people in black and white hats and trying to keep track of what imaginary people might infer about the inferences of other imaginary people. It was only when, hours later, the light began to dim and the rain eased to a stop that I had the answer.

Arnaud pulled on his brakes when it came to me and, naturally, I assumed he had read my mind.

'OK, so I think I've got it,' I said, stopping behind him.

'Got it? Got what?'

'The answer to the brain teaser.'

'*Quoi?*'

'The bran teezar.'

'Ah, *bon*! So, what is it?'

I told him my answer.

'Aha, *c'est bon*! Well done! I 'ave more for you, but I think now we should stop being in our heads,' he said, motioning towards the sea. At the tip of a long cove, crystal water caressed the empty sand of Storvika beach.

The cove was enclosed by mountain ridges, which, in the distance, merged with the Atlantic and with the pastel hues of the sky.

'Shall we stop 'ere a while?'

'Yeah, I think we have to,' I said, realising this was one of those places that makes your soul simmer.

We walked our bikes beside a stream that ran into the sea. On the edge of the sand was a picnic bench. We sat facing the water and the mountains and the kaleidoscopic sky. Instinctively, we began nodding; nothing we might say could do justice to what we were seeing; all we could do was let each other know we were seeing it too.

I pulled two cans of beer out of a pannier and handed one to Arnaud.

'Cheers,' I said, holding my can towards his.

'*Santé*,' he replied.

We glugged down some of the ice-cold beer.

'I think it's a good time for something else, too,' said Arnaud, tapping the breast pocket of his jacket and grinning.

'What do you have there?'

He set his beer down on the bench, undid the zipper on his pocket, then pulled out a poorly rolled joint, all loose and wonky.

I smiled. 'You roll that yourself?'

'Oui,' he replied, at first looking indignant, then smiling too. 'You want it or not?'

I shrugged.

As smoke drifted into the cool air towards the horizon, we talked about our first times cycle touring. Mine was before I even knew it was a thing. There was a music festival in Cornwall, about 300 kilometres from home. A few friends were driving there, but I'd just bought a new bike, something for getting around town, and thought I might cycle there instead. I set off in jeans and flip-flops, and with my clothes and rations in a backpack. I spent my first night on the cold stones of a desolate beach and my second day on the hard shoulder of a motorway. My arse hurt so much while riding that I folded up my spare clothes and inserted them into the backside of my jeans. After three lonely days, I arrived at the festival, exhausted and visibly thinner.

Arnaud's first trip was from Geneva to Istanbul on a tandem bike. At 18, he was a couple of years older than his cycling companion, who had somehow convinced their teachers to let them do the ride for a school project. Neither had ever ridden a tandem or had been abroad without their parents. But after a long summer of sleeping beneath bridges, encounters with snarling Bosnian dogs and swigs of Serbian vodka, they finally rolled into Istanbul.

It was the best of times, it was the worst of times. Sometimes yes, sometimes no.

Predictably, our minds turned to food. We agreed to cycle for an hour more, find somewhere to camp, then make spaghetti on Arnaud's burner.

The final stretch of the day began with a long tunnel that had large ventilation fans on the ceiling. In my 'altered state of consciousness', they were as loud as jet engines. Their whirring, along with the sounds of trucks and cars, reverberated up and down the tunnel, and was so thick I felt I might float up off of the road and drift through the air to the end of the tunnel. The blackness, interrupted only by the industrial yellow lights, contrasted dramatically with the blues and greens of the sea and trees when I emerged on the other side. Sure, I had seen blues and greens before, though not quite these shades, I was sure.

But not everybody was seeing the world in technicolour. An old grey Volvo pulled over ahead of us and a woman jumped out, clutching a fluorescent vest. She held it out for Arnaud to take. 'Please, one of you needs to wear this,' she said. 'I almost drove into you.' Deprived of logic, Arnaud and I glanced at the surrounding landscapes to confirm whether they were as bright as we perceived them to be. '*D'accord*,' said Arnaud and put on the vest. The woman, seeming flustered, strode back to her car and drove off.

Arnaud was less particular than me about where he camped. I always wanted to be as far as possible from people; I felt, for some reason, that I had to conceal what I was up to. Maybe it was more fun that way, as if I was on some sort of covert operation. When we came across a seaside campsite, he suggested we venture in, even though he had no intention of paying to stay there. This seemed foolish to me, but I played along. We coasted around the grounds, waving to strolling campers, until Arnaud came to a sudden stop by a small section of grass beside a slipway.

'This,' he said, pointing to the grass. 'This will do nicely.'

'You're serious?' I asked. 'You wanna just stay in the campsite without paying?'

'*Non*,' he said, 'I want to stay *next* to this campsite without paying.'

He stamped on the ground. 'This little track, I think is the edge of the campsite. *Oui*, everything around us is the campsite, but this little bit of grass, I think *non*.'

I had no idea how he'd reached this conclusion and told him as much.

'*Excusez moi, monsieur!*' he called out to a passing man, who had come from a part of the campsite for long-term guests. 'This 'ere, it is part of the campsite?'

The man looked at us uneasily. 'Well, no,' he began, 'but…'

'*Merci!*' said Arnaud, cutting him off.

The man plodded away and Arnaud looked at me. 'Well, then, shall we get set up?'

I sighed. 'OK, why not?'

'*Exactement*,' replied Arnaud, 'why not?'

With our tents pitched, we made ourselves at home on the little patch of no man's land, which had its own picnic bench. Soon, Arnaud had seawater boiling and a thick bundle of spaghetti in his hands, which he snapped in two and dropped in. When it was cooked, he drained the water, poured in some pasta sauce, stirred it, then served the spaghetti in two plastic bowls. *Bon appétit.*

Still a little high, we ate with gusto, washing the spaghetti down with beer. Occasionally, we'd return the stares of long-term guests, who were displeased we'd found a way of enjoying the campsite without paying for it. With mouths full of spaghetti, we'd laugh victoriously when the disgruntled person disappeared. We amused ourselves like this until the mosquitoes came to join the party, then retreated to our tents.

In the morning, we passed through a dark tunnel, which reminded Arnaud about the fluorescent vest we'd been given by the woman in the Volvo. The moment he put it on, she drove past us, with a thumb up and a big grin.

An hour later we saw her again at a petrol station café that had been recommended to us by an American cyclist. We were drinking coffee and scoffing waffles when she came over. She told us she'd once hitchhiked the length of the country with her new-born son and had learned then that the roads could be dangerous, but also that she could rely on the generosity of strangers. After seeing us the previous evening, she'd felt guilty that she hadn't offered us her garden to camp in. With a sombre face and her hand on her heart, she made us promise we'd be careful, then marched back to her car. It seemed something traumatic had once happened to her on the road, but we never discovered what.

We merged with a stream of cyclists when we left the café: this was the last stretch of the 17. We were almost in Bodø – the gateway to Lofoten. Filled with caffeine and sugar, we pedalled hard, pausing only on Saltstraumen Bridge, where we marvelled at the swirling blue and white water below. With 400 million cubic metres of water forcing its way through a channel of just 150 metres every six hours, the Saltstraumen strait is home to the strongest tidal currents in the world. The water, which flows between Saltfjord (to the west) and Skjerstad Fjord (to the east) at up to 40 kph is dotted with whirlpools, some 10 metres wide and 5 deep.

It began to rain as we entered the suburbs of Bodø, where we contended with the joys of urban cycling – traffic lights and traffic, construction and diversions, exhaust pipes and exhaustion. But the centre of the little Arctic city was quiet and we zipped through its streets towards the ferry terminal, then staggered inside, perspiring, to check the timetable. As we tried to make sense of it, we heard the horn of a ship. I pointed to a number. 18.45. Arnaud looked at his wrist. '*Merde!*' He held his watch for me to see. 18.50. There wouldn't be another ferry until 03.15 the next morning.

We plodded back outside to our bikes.

'Well, what to do for the next eight hours?' Arnaud asked, rubbing his hands together. 'Shall we find somewhere to cook some spaghetti?'

I glanced up at the dull sky and imagined us in a damp park, huddling beside his little burner.

'No, man, let's celebrate somewhere. This is Bodø. I can't believe we're here. Didn't it always look like it was forever away?'

He nodded. '*Oui*, I know what you mean.'

We got back on our bikes and went in search of a restaurant. We rolled along grey and damp commercial streets, weaving between pedestrians, until exotic scents filled my nostrils. I pulled on my brakes to stop and sniff. 'How about here?' I asked, sticking my thumb in the direction of a sign, already excited by what I might find inside.

'Great Gandhi,' said Arnaud, reading the words slowly. He shrugged his shoulders. 'When in Rome, I suppose?' he continued with a smirk. 'You don't want some pickled herring? A little dried cod?'

I had already opened the door and was basking in the spicy warmth.

A well-dressed Norwegian-Indian led us to some plush seats and a window-side table with a white cloth, lavish napkins and intricate silverware, overlooked by a purple image of Gandhi.

As is customary in Indian restaurants, I ordered far more than I could possibly consume – poppadoms, mango chutney, bhajis, samosas, coconut rice, korma, peshwari naan – then ate in a state of ecstasy until I felt like a balloon.

Throughout, we kept an eye on the sky. Gradually, the clouds were clearing, revealing a silk sheet of crimson.

'You know, we only smoked 'alf of that joint,' said Arnaud, looking through the window at some fishing boats in a harbour. He checked his watch. 'And we still 'ave six hours to kill. What do you think's on the other side of that 'arbour?' he asked, tapping a finger on the window.

We paid up, climbed back on our bikes and rode towards the fishing boats, where seagulls perched on stone benches, quivering in the breeze. Beyond the harbour was a park and beyond that was a small beach, dotted with red huts.

We sat on a picnic bench facing the sea; I pulled two beers from a pannier and Arnaud lit up the half-smoked joint.

Connected to the beach by a path of rocks was a small island that looked like a turtle. The more we smoked, the more it seemed as if it was swimming towards us, backlit by a glowing sky, with modest trees growing from its shell.

'I think we 'ave to go say 'ello to 'im,' said Arnaud, nodding and wearing a goofy grin.

'Yeah, I think so too,' I replied, nodding and grinning in the same way.

We stood, waited for the dizziness to subside, then stomped across the seaweed-covered sand to the rock path. Halfway across, Arnaud stopped suddenly. 'OK,' he said, 'but we 'ave to remember to keep an eye on this path.' We had seen a stray dinghy wash up on the beach, so knew the tide was coming in. I thought he was worrying about nothing. 'I think we'll be OK,' I said, dismissively.

We clambered up the turtle's shell – clumps of grass in one hand, beer in the other – then walked over to the far side and sat on a rock. There were hundreds more islands in the distance, the largest among them the nature reserve of Bliksvær about 12 kilometres west.

We sat sipping beer and admiring the islands, until I noticed Arnaud had his backpack of valuables by his side. *Damn*, I thought, *I left all my things on the beach. Wallet, passport, laptop, camera, drone – all just sitting there.* 'I've gotta go back to the beach quickly,' I told Arnaud. 'Need to get my things.'

'*D'accord,*' said Arnaud, blowing a plume of smoke into the evening air, then taking a sip of beer.

I got up, then made my way back to the head of the turtle. As I lowered myself to begin scrambling down the edge of his shell, I noticed something was missing. Where the path of rocks had been, there was now an expanse of silver water.

I strode back to Arnaud, who was still smoking serenely.

'You were right,' I said.

'About what?'

'Keeping an eye on the path.'

For a brief moment, he wore an expression of shock, though this was quickly replaced by one of glee.

'I knew it!' he said, excitedly climbing to his feet and picking up his backpack. He was thrilled to have been right about the perils of the tide.

When we reached the water's edge, we saw that a few of the larger rocks were still piercing the surface of the water and that some were barely beneath it. By leaping between these, we made it back to the beach without the water soaking anything besides our shoes and socks.

'I knew it!' said Arnaud again as we walked back to our bikes.

It was now getting late and we were ready to sleep, so headed for the terminal and joined a few others stretched out on the floor and across rows of plastic seats. I drifted off to the sounds of men snoring and of Arnaud, whose eating was normally strictly regimented, binge-eating peanut butter sandwiches.

I awoke to those feelings of anger and agony that accompany early alarms. *The boat'll be here soon,* I told myself, my eyes still shut, my duck-inspired alarm still quacking. *Gotta get up.* I rubbed my eyes, stood, then prodded

Arnaud's shoulder with my toe. 'We gotta go.' He went through the same emotions and motions I had, then climbed to his feet.

We wheeled our bikes into the never-ending daylight, then stood by a large ramp at the front of a long line of cars. When the ferry drifted in over the glistening water, we boarded, each found a flat, cushioned bench, then resumed our respective slumbers.

It was still early morning when we arrived Moskenes, a municipality at the southern tip of the Lofoten archipelago. It was overcast and windswept. A few old, wooden buildings were scattered around the bleak terminal.

Arnaud was diligent about washing every morning, so headed straight for a cabin that served as a public toilet. His ablutions involved getting fully naked, covering himself in soap, then rinsing himself off. Since he would only have hand soap and a little metallic basin, this seemed an unpleasant and arduous task to undertake at the ferry terminal. At least the cabin was comprised of private cubicles and contained no communal areas, so he wouldn't get caught starkers by an unsuspecting dock worker.

Still half asleep, I leant on my bike as I waited for him outside. I was mid-yawn when the door swung open and Arnaud returned, looking pleased with himself.

'You are tired, *oui*?'

I nodded and yawned again. 'Yes. *Oui.*'

'So, you're not against taking a nap?'

I shook my head. '*Non.* I'm not against it.'

'*C'est bon.* Let's take a little ride up there,' said Arnaud, pointing to the road north, 'and see what we can find.'

I nodded again and swung a heavy leg over my bike. We rode until we came across a flat patch of grass at the top of a cliff, then quickly set up our tents, eager to escape the dreary weather and to return to dreams once more.

The sun snuck into the sky as we slept, and by early afternoon its warmth had coaxed us from our tents. Rested and with the archipelago we had long fantasised about now dappled in light, we dismantled our tents with the same urgency with which we'd set them up, then marched back to the road.

Mesmerised by the landscapes, we pointed out things to each other as we cycled in single file. With our words lost in the breeze, we never quite understood what the other was pointing to, but it didn't matter. 'Look!' Arnaud would say, his finger directed towards something in the distance. I'd smile and nod. *Maybe it's those mountains he likes. Like rows of sharp teeth. Or those huts on stilts in the water.* 'Check that out!' I'd say, tilting my head towards sections of the sea like turquoise glass, so clear you could watch the yellow weeds swaying on the seabed. Arnaud would glance in the general direction, then smile and nod.

As we approached the village of Hamnøy, what seemed to be a triangular thatched cottage came into view, but something about it wasn't quite right. We stared at the structure as we edged towards the settlement, trying to determine what exactly about it was odd. Then the answer came to us over the wind – the smell of death. The structure's brown exterior wasn't made of straw or reeds, but of thousands of fish heads. We stopped to take a closer look. The heads still wore the horror-filled expressions they had when plucked from the water. These fish, I later learned, would have been caught in the winter; drying them in cold air is an ancient preservation method that ensures fishing communities don't go hungry when the fish swim elsewhere.

'Funny,' said Arnaud, without elaboration.

'What is?'

'All these fish and not a single bird.'

'Hmm, yeah, that is strange.'

Each holding a sleeve over our noses and mouths, we stared at the terror-stricken heads a little more, then shrugged. *Maybe it's not so strange that not even the birds want anything to do with this.*

We turned around to admire the landscape we had just cycled through. Beside us, red wooden houses perched on flat rocks at the edge of a fjord. Across the mirror-like water, angular, snow-capped mountains punctured the pale blue sky. Overlooking the fish heads, Lofoten really was as magnificent as it had seemed in all the pictures I had pored over months before.

We looked at each other and nodded.

'Feel like some spaghetti?' asked Arnaud.

'Sure.'

'But not right here,' he said, glancing at the fish heads.

'No, not here.'

In the village, we followed a track to some grass. In the centre, among cow parsley and small yellow flowers was an old iron table. It overlooked a large expanse of still blue water, beyond which was a dark ridge of jagged mountains.

I stood on a rock at the water's edge as Arnaud got set up on the table.

'I think it looks warmer than it is,' he said, reading my mind.

I smiled, impressed by his perceptiveness. 'But it's not getting any warmer,' I replied, then crouched down and splashed the sunlit water with my fingers. 'How many more chances will I have to swim in the Arctic Circle? Plus, if I do it now, at least I'll have hot spaghetti to eat afterwards.'

'This is true,' said Arnaud as he lit his burner.

Still crouched and with my fingers dangling in the sea, I deliberated some more. I thought about where we were relative to other places in the world. At 68 degrees north, we were far closer to the Pole than places like Anchorage and Iceland.

Arnaud walked towards me with his pan, into which he put a little sea water. 'You're thinking about it too much now,' he said, but then dipped a finger into the pan and grimaced as if in pain.

'You're right,' I said, standing up. 'It's the perfect time.' I walked over to the table, stripped down to my boxer shorts, retrieved a dry pair and my towel from a pannier, then laid them on the table to warm in the sunlight. I took a deep breath, then, more slowly, walked back to the water. The rocks were slippery, so I squatted down and put my hands behind me, clambering forwards like a physically challenged crab. When I reached the edge of a large rock next to a section of deep water I stood, took another deep breath, then dove in.

Immediately, the cold tore the air from my body, as if fists were clenched around my lungs. Despite my urgent need to breathe, the momentum of my dive pulled me further underwater, towards the yellow weeds I had admired from the road. From here, their dancing betrayed sinister intentions, like the twinkle in a mermaid's eye. Unable to stop, I slid into the weeds, which caressed my face, then chest, then legs. When I finally came to a halt, I took a stroke to propel myself back to the surface, which suddenly seemed very far above. I let out an inaudible cry and with it my remaining breath. Tauntingly, the bubbles raced past me. I felt the weeds under my foot. I kicked lest they try wrap themselves around my ankle, pushed off the seabed and shot upwards.

I gasped as my head breached the surface. A chuckle came from the shore, though it barely registered. As fast as I could, I swam back to the rocks, frantically staggered out and dashed towards my towel, which I wrapped around my shoulders.

'It was nice?' asked Arnaud, smirking, as he poured sauce onto the spaghetti.

I didn't respond. I just sat down and leant over the sunlit table. When the shivering subsided, I stood and got dressed.

'You know,' said Arnaud as I pulled my cycling shorts back on, 'this'll be our last time eating together.'

'Oh, yeah?'

'*Oui*, I looked up where my friend lives and it's not far from 'ere. Just a few hours.' He added some pepper to the spaghetti, then continued. 'But, if you want, maybe I can ask 'im if you can stay too?'

I thought about it for a moment. 'Thanks, but I need to keep covering ground.' In reality, I was doing fine for time. I had about a week to complete the remaining 500 kilometres to Tromsø. I didn't want to impose, is all.

'*D'accord.*'

Filled with spaghetti, we set off on our last ride together. The road followed the winding coastline and I thought back to meeting Marco and Ida and how they'd described the sea in this part of the country as 'unreal'. It was true; the cyan waters that flowed into the coves and that lapped at the white-sand shores didn't belong in a place like this. But it was the contrasts – Caribbean seas and Arctic mountains – that made Lofoten special. At the northern edge of one island, we entered Nappstraum Tunnel and plunged 60 metres below the sea, then worked up a sweat climbing out the other side. Arnaud wiped his brow as we pulled over by the exit. 'It's over there somewhere, across that bridge,' he said, referring to his friend's farm. Slowly, we rode towards and over the modest bridge, which crossed a narrow inlet. 'OK, it's down this track. You're sure you don't want to stay a while? I'm sure my friend wouldn't mind.'

Yes, I told him; I had to keep going.

We thanked each other for the company, hugged, then went our separate ways.

I was struck by how familiar and distinct being alone felt. It was as though there were two souls inside of me; when I'd met Arnaud, one had vanished and the other had appeared, and now they had switched places again. This was the one that I knew best, the one that had been there for the first few weeks of the ride. It was the one that harboured a loneliness it dared not acknowledge, but that also relished solitude and the freedom it represented – to go slow, to go fast, to stop, to stare, to be quiet.

I didn't sleep much that night. In a campsite brimming with drunk Russians, I pitched beside a small lake. There was a plunge pool and a jacuzzi beside it. Until the early hours of the morning, the jovial Russians alternated between the two, shrieking as they braved the former and singing in chorus while in the latter. When their vodka finally ran dry, they retreated, slurring, to their campervans. In the relative quiet, I heard the wind howling down the valley. My tent quivered when it reached the campsite some moments later. This pattern – the sound of the distant wind, followed by the flapping of my tent – repeated itself over or over, each time with greater ferocity, until pegs started to pop out of the ground. At five in the morning, I crawled outside and began collecting rocks to hold down the section of the flysheet that faced the wind. With these in place, I drove a few more pegs into the ground, tied a guyline to my bike, then crawled back inside for a few hours of uneasy sleep.

The next day, without Arnaud to talk to, I listened to podcasts as I followed the southern coast of Vestvågøya, one of the more substantial islands of Lofoten at about 400 square kilometres. I crossed a bridge to little Gimsøya, then another to large Austvågøy, whose winding west coast I followed south. Those unreal blues filled a little cove at Rørvikstranda, where an elderly couple strode soberly into the water I had only briefly managed to tolerate the day before. At the bottom of Austvågøy, the road skipped across a few islets, before ending in the village of Henningsvær, which itself straddles a pair of tiny islands.

Being at the end of a road, Henningsvær – comprised of a few streets, houses and simple shops – never used to receive many visitors. It's only since the spread of consumer drones that tourists have really started to arrive. The reason is a football pitch. Located on a rocky outcrop that holds nothing else besides some wooden frames for drying fish, the bright green pitch looks otherworldly from above, surrounded by deep blue water. Having a drone myself, the pitch was, admittedly, the reason I had made the detour to Henningsvær.

Arriving at the pitch, however, there was a queue to stand on the centre spot and to have one's photo taken from above, so I instead climbed a hillock and had a fly around from there. Having acquired evidence of my presence by the famous pitch, I hopped on my bike, then headed back to Austvågøy.

It was the sea that kept me awake that night. After a couple of hours cycling west along the southern coast of Austvågøy, I spotted an empty beach, where I decided to camp. A steep bank led to the beach. Beyond, a dozen islets slept in an orange sea. Rather than take my bike down the bank, I hung it with my lock to a tree, then completed several trips, carrying a few bags each time. Next, I set about deciding where to pitch. A tent-sized indent among some large rocks caught my eye. It was some way back from the water, though I noticed the rocks had two distinct shades – darker at the bottom than at the top. Likewise, the sand in the indent was darker than at the back of the beach. I recalled my and Arnaud's escape from the turtle-shaped island in Bodø, where the tide had changed so much in so little time, and abandoned the indent in favour of setting up at the back of the beach.

It was at midnight that the sloshing sounds snuck into my dreams, becoming louder and louder until my eyes shot open. I reached for the zip of my tent and undid it slowly, afraid of what I might find. The sea was still orange beneath the sun, but the islets were long gone. While I couldn't have hit the water with a stone when I pitched, it was now just a few strides from the edge of my tent. In the partial darkness, I reminded myself that I had definitely seen a line in the sand and that I had set up behind this, though I couldn't help but think I might have overlooked something. I packed my bags in case I needed to make a quick escape and, with this precaution taken, slept some more.

But still the sloshing found its way into my consciousness and I awoke again two hours later. This time the water was scarcely a metre from my tent. It occurred to me then that I could look up the local tides. One website said high tide was at 02.45, in 45 minutes. To estimate how much further the water might reach, I tried to imagine where it had been when I had first woken up a couple of hours earlier. In 45 minutes, I guessed, it'll be touching the tips of my shoes, which were in the porch outside the tent proper. I stuck my head into the cool air. The indent in the rocks I had thought about pitching in was under a half metre of water.

I left the flysheet unzipped and stared at the encroaching sea and at my watch. As the tide crept ever closer, I thought about packing up. *No*, said my rational mind, struggling to get my attention among the images of water pouring into my tent, *there was a line in the sand*. At 02.30, the sea was grasping at the peg nearest to it, but it was apparent by then that only a freak wave would result in the water getting to me and my belongings. As 02.45 became 03.00, the clasping white fingers were gradually drawn backwards. And just as the moon drew the sea it made heavy my eyelids and pulled me back into unconsciousness.

The islets had reappeared by the time I clambered out of my tent and began packing up. Some were now even accessible by paths of sand. The narrow strip I had slept on was once more a broad beach, which I plodded along until I reached the bank that led to the road.

I followed the coast of Sloverfjord, where flocks of gulls drifted in silence over the surface of the water, escorting me on my last few hours in Lofoten. From the village of Fiskebøl, I took a ferry to the small island of Hadseløya, the southernmost member of the Vesterålen archipelago. With green hills, lakes, and coastal roads, Hadseløya was perfectly nice, but had nothing I really wanted to see. *Lonely Planet* has this to say of it: 'Of all the Vesterålen islands, this is the one where you're likely to spend the least time.'

On the north side of Hadseløya, the curving, kilometre-long Hasdel Bridge led me to the larger island of Langøya. Beneath a blanket of grey skies, Langøya's modest hills were draped in forests and farmland. It was another fine island, but it wasn't hard to see why the more dynamic Lofoten was the golden child of these twin archipelagos.

I saw so few people on Langøya that I remember them all. There was a couple on touring bikes heading the other way. We waved and smiled at each other – knowing waves, knowing smiles; sometimes yes, sometimes no. Later, at a fork in the road, I had stopped to check my map when I heard a distant voice. I looked all around until I spotted a man in a garden across the road. He held up his secateurs and used them to point. 'Go that way,' he called. 'There's a big hill the other way.' The last person I interacted with that day was a man in a car. He yelled something out of his window as he passed and pointed to a decrepit cycle lane I had opted not to use, in case I broke another wheel. Besides, there was plenty of room on the road. Suppressing my primal reaction to being yelled at, I gave him a thumbs up in his mirror, then hopped onto the cycle lane until he was out of sight. He was the first motorist in 2,000 kilometres to have shown me any ill will, and for that I was grateful.

With little to occupy my senses, I spent the afternoon pondering the third of three problems Arnaud had given me. This one also involved hats. Twenty people were in a room wearing either a black one or a white one. Each person can see the hats of the others, though can't see their own. This is a dilemma, because their lives depend on figuring out the colour of their own hat. (Evidently, they're all participants in a sick game orchestrated by some puzzle-loving sadist.) All they're allowed to say is, 'the colour of my hat is black' or, 'the colour of my hat is white.' However, before entering the room, they meet with you to discuss what they'll do once in there. How many people can you save and how?

I thought about these people in hats, imagining them in various formations, until it dawned on me that I should find somewhere to spend the night. As uncultivated land was scarce, I looked up campsites. There was one just outside the town of Sortland, on the east coast of Langøya. 'You're better off washing in a stream,' said one review, referring to the campsite's showers. 'Dingy and neglected... an absolute scandal,' said another. The campsite was, however, the only one around, so I reluctantly made my way there. Sure enough, it was a little worse for wear, with bits of tarp and wood strewn over the grass and a urinal that perpetually sprayed water over the floor. I had managed, however, to pick up a replacement for my punctured air mattress at a supermarket, so was content inside my tent, catching up on sleep after two restless nights.

In the morning I drew a meandering line across Sortland Bridge, pushed off course by a strong wind. As I reached the island of Hinnøya, where I turned north, it began to rain. By the time I made it to Andøya, the northernmost island in the Vesterålen archipelago, I was being pummelled by a howling headwind and icy rain. As I often did when the weather was bad, I took my breaks in bus shelters. The damp shelters on Andøya, however, were brimming with mosquitoes, and it was hard to choose between being drained of blood or spending more time outside in the Norwegian summer.

I kept my head down as I pushed forward through the wind and rain, turning my attention inwards to picture more favourable worlds: palm trees and piña coladas, or bed, coffee and peanut butter on toast. But wherever I fantasised about, people in black and white hats would show up. 'You haven't figured out how to save us yet,' they'd say. 'You're right,' I'd reply, then would get back to work, occasionally having moments of insight, but always reaching an impasse.

When I did look up, I saw a brown and weather-beaten landscape, where hardy shrubs and small trees clung to the wet ground, lest they be sucked by the tempest into the sky. Headlands projected into turbulent grey seas, covered in a thick haze, as if what lay beyond was not intended for human eyes. When this world had siphoned most of my energy, I scoured it for places to sleep, but I had read that Andøya was known for a certain type of land and it was clear that it was all around me: bog. Endless stretches of flat ground, all of it thoroughly saturated with water. Bog is to the camper as the ocean is to the dehydrated.

I made it to Stave Camping and Hot Pools in the evening, by which time the weather had almost worn itself out, and different shades of Andøya were emerging. In one of the outdoor jacuzzis there was a family, shrouded in steam, enjoying views of bright green grass, white sand and clear, blue sea. Having spent too much time in the great outdoors, I made do with a quick shower, then retreated to my tent for the night, where I stared at my nylon ceiling and thought about how to save the people in hats. When a potential answer came to me, I sent it to Arnaud, then went to sleep.

I awoke, smiling, to the sound of gentle waves and to sunlight warming my tent. I smiled wider when I recalled seeing a fancy coffee machine in the reception. I got dressed and marched over there, my plastic bag of breakfast supplies swinging in my hand. 'Looks like a nice day,' I said to the Finnish woman as she made my coffee. She agreed and said that sun was forecast for the next few days.

I could have wept.

'Mind you,' she said, as she slid my coffee over the desk, 'I'm worried it's going to be *too* hot. Supposed to get to seventeen degrees today.'

I stifled a smirk, the type people from hot places had given me when I told them that, actually, it can get up to *25* degrees in England in summer.

'Wow, *seventeen*? Maybe I'll take my jacket off today!'

I took my coffee to a picnic bench and made myself a sandwich. I searched my memories. It was the first time I had had breakfast outside since arriving in Norway. Every single morning I had eaten inside my tent.

When I returned my cup, I asked the receptionist if there was anything to see in Stave. She recommended a short hike to a nearby beach – where I could take a dip if I felt myself overheating.

At the trail head, I locked my bike to a fence, removed my panniers and got to hiking. People were outnumbered by sheep on the grassy hills and it was often hard to tell whether the tracks had been left by the former or the latter. But when the path I took ended on the side of a cliff, I concluded that its creator was likely not of the bipedal variety. Since I had a pannier in each hand, mimicking the locomotive strategy of the sheep was not an option, so I turned back, abandoning my intention of making it to the beach. Again, however, by walking along a ledge that gradually narrowed, I reached a dead end. A woman's voice came from behind me as I stood with my face pressed against a rock and a large drop below. She repeated herself in English when I didn't respond.

'Can I take your bags for you?'

I don't know, I thought, *can you?* I had no real idea of how far from me she was. 'If you can,' I said, turning my neck just enough so that I wasn't talking directly into the rock, but not so much that I might lose my balance.

'OK,' she said, 'don't move. I'll climb up a bit.'

I felt my left pannier wobble. 'Alright, you can let that one go,' came the voice. 'OK, now let go of this one,' she said again a moment later. 'If you can turn around, there's a rock you can climb down onto.'

I turned my neck some more, then slowly my body and legs, being sure to keep my centre of gravity over the ledge. As she had said, there was a large rock about a metre below. I leapt onto it and then slid down until my feet touched the ground.

I thanked the woman as she handed my panniers back to me.

'You're very welcome,' she said. 'Are you a cyclist?'

'Yep, on my way to Tromsø. Should be there in a few days.'

'Well,' she continued, looking up at the sky, 'it's a good day for it. Supposed to get up to *seventeen* today!'

While I had retreated from the elements into my mind the previous day, the sun now had me looking out in wonder at this curious corner of Norway. After outrunning a posse of flies that chased me from the trailhead along the road, I arrived in the village of Bleik, where one of the longest white-sand beaches in the country is flanked by swaying green grasses and lapping turquoise waters. Shortly after, I passed a rocket range, of all things. (I later read that a rocket from Andøya Space Centre, built to collect data on the aurora borealis, almost led to nuclear war. Launched in 1995, shortly after the Cold War, it was mistaken by the Russians as an American missile. Anticipating that Moscow might be struck in a matter of minutes, the nuclear briefcase was brought to then-president Boris Yeltsin and the commanders of Russian submarines prepared to retaliate. Ultimately, radar operators determined the rocket was heading away from Russian airspace and the submarine commanders relaxed their trigger fingers. It's the only known incident of a nuclear-weapons state preparing to launch an attack.) Just north of the rocket range I passed by Andøya Airport, outside of which were military barricades and a young woman with an assault rifle, who smiled and said hi.

I arrived at Andenes ferry terminal on the northern tip of Andøya in mid afternoon. Checking the timetable, I learned the next boat to Senja wouldn't arrive for another two hours. The sun was still out and I happily passed the time on a picnic bench, looking through photos of all the places I'd seen – the hiking trails to Trolltunga, the curvaceous bridges of Atlantic Ocean Road, the teeth-like mountains of Lofoten. But my favourite part of Norway was yet to come.

Nordland Statistics

- Distance (trip total): 817 kilometres (2,135 kilometres)

- Climbing (trip total): 8,394 metres (26,455 metres)

- Highest point: 346 metres (FV17, northeast of Nesna)

- Island Rides project distance: 4,619 kilometres

- Island Rides project climbing: 46,338 metres

Troms

From my rotting body, flowers shall grow and I am in them and that is eternity.

Edvard Munch, Norwegian painter

I loved Senja as soon as I saw it. I rolled off the ferry and onto the island in the early evening. The road passed through a hamlet, just a few wooden houses at the end of a headland, then followed the coast of a narrow fjord, its edges marked by steep mountains and forests of emerald. I hadn't thought it possible that anywhere could feel more remote than some of the places I had seen in Norway; but Senja did. On average, Norway is home to just seventeen people per square kilometre, but on Senja there are only five. Outside the distant archipelago of Svalbard, Senja is, at 1,500 square kilometres, the second largest island in Norway, with a population of less than 8,000. Arriving was like that moment you notice the fridge stop humming; 'Oh,' you think, '*this* is silence.'

The island has certain idiosyncrasies that seemed apt for such a quiet place. Less frequent was the pale blue of Lofoten and Vesterålen, replaced by waters of deep navy, wherein islands dwelt, some occupied by old houses, accessed by boat or bridge. Like the fjords, the tunnels were darker too. After two hours in Senja, I reached the top of an ascent, where a small lake reflected the snow of the surrounding peaks and an ominous, downhill tunnel began. With only dim, flickering bulbs hanging from a cable on the ceiling and my bike equipped with the type of lights made for being seen rather than for seeing, I could scarcely make out the tunnel walls as I plummeted, my brakes screeching in the cold, damp air.

Having escaped the tunnel, I wound down the road until I spotted the Bergsbotn viewing platform, a sleek wooden structure jutting out into the air above a hairpin turn overlooking Bergsfjord. From here, it seemed just a couple of small settlements interrupted the long, green shores of the fjord, with the road running alongside. There were headlands poking into the water that would make idyllic campsites, and I continued towards them.

As I approached one of the headlands, I couldn't believe my luck that someone hadn't yet built a house on it. I coasted to a stop, then ploughed my way through the thick vegetation between the road and the shore. I dropped my bike and my backpack in the long grass when I reached the water, then stood still a while to admire the contours of the surrounding mountains and their reflections in the fjord. I took a moment to close my eyes too; almost as exquisite as the views was the silence.

As the sun warmed my tent the following morning, I looked at the map and calculated how far it was to Tromsø. I was shocked by the result; it was only another 110 kilometres (and there were three full days until my flight home). *I'm basically there!* This made me very happy as it meant I would no longer have to ride past the point of enjoying it; if I saw something of interest, I could stop and look; I could even go to see Segla, the mountain Marco had described as an alien fortress. It was best seen from Mt Hesten, which was only a few hours away, overlooking the village of Fjordgård.

It was a fine morning and I was eager to enjoy it. To the lapping of the sparkling fjord and the chirping of small birds, I struck my tent, then cycled to the local supermarket. Compounding my excitement, there was free coffee, to which I added some chocolate milk. Caffeinated, I sped along the coast, instinctively urging myself onwards, until it occurred to me that there was no need. In fact, I should slow down; it would be nice to see Segla in the evening light. At Tungeneset viewpoint, I admired a headland that resembled a serrated knife, and passed the time reading on a sunlit rock beside the sea.

When a band of flies discovered my location, I continued, passing by Ersfjord beach, where a hundred tourists had gathered on the grassy dunes and were sitting in campervans or setting up tents. Shortly after, riding through a long tunnel, I talked out loud to myself about the people in hats, having just received a negative response from Arnaud about my latest solution. I cut short my conversation when I noticed two young women with backpacks walking towards me, amused to have caught me thinking I was alone. Beyond the tunnel, the road followed the winding coastline, then headed inland and uphill. My mustiness lured swarms of flies towards me as I ascended, unable to go fast enough to escape them as they hitched a ride on my handlebars, hands and ears. It was only when I reached a descent that I outran them, though still one found its way into my eye and I had to use my phone's camera to locate it and then dig it out with a finger.

As I approached the final stretch to Fjordgård, I entered what has been described in local papers as the 'horror tunnel'. In winter, huge slabs of ice form on its ceiling and are prone to falling onto those passing through. When I arrived, work had begun to prevent this and to replace the road's surface. This meant the ceiling – where the lights normally were – and the tarmac had been stripped. Armed only with my little front light, I could make out the ground just in front of me, but nothing more – not the upcoming potholes or the tunnel walls. I realised at one point, progressing at a crawl, I hadn't any idea how long the tunnel was. All I knew was the daylight from behind was long gone and the end was nowhere to be seen. Some tunnels had taken half an hour to ride through, which would seem an eternity in the pitch black of this one. As I started to imagine a lone astronaut slipping from his ship and into space, I heard a car behind, and then saw my shadow on the rough ground. *Yes!* I stood and began pedalling hard, desperate to keep the car behind me so it would light my way. I was gasping for breath when the bright pinhole of the tunnel's end appeared. Grateful, I shot out into the fresh air, to be welcomed by the head of a deep blue fjord.

Almost immediately, however, I spotted the entrance to another dark and narrow tunnel. I looked at the map to check its length; it was several times longer than the one I'd just passed through. Foolishly, I did a search for 'Fjordgårdtunnelen' on my phone and was greeted by images of anxious locals standing by piles of snow, ice-covered walls and dangling cables. It had recently been rated the most dangerous tunnel on Senja. I edged towards it, trying to delay what seemed inevitable. But as I neared its ravenous mouth, I spotted something. A track. There was another way. I bumped along the dirt track, which ran alongside the fjord for 2 kilometres before re-joining the road.

Shortly after, I entered Fjordgård, where a flock of squawking terns spiralled over the wooden houses. On the side of one little road was the trailhead to Mt Hesten, marked by a modest shelter. I put my valuables, a carton of orange juice and some nuts into my backpack, left everything else by the shelter and locked my bike to a post, then began up the trail. Ahead, Segla shot into the sky, like a giant canine tooth towering 600 metres above the village.

It didn't take the Senja flies long to rediscover my location. I tried to ignore them and even let a few take a brief ride on my forearms. That's when I met 'the big bastards' and learned that some of the island's flies bite. As one sunk its fangs into my skin, I swatted at it, landing a clean blow. I watched it quiver on the ground for a moment, then raised my foot. As I was about to stamp, I had a change of heart, then set my foot back down, next to the grape-sized fly. 'Tell your friends,' I said, hoping to spread news of my mercy. (Admittedly, I also said this to flies to whom I showed no mercy, hoping that news of my fury might do the rounds.) It made no difference. I felt like a walking corpse as I plodded onwards, engulfed by my insect companions. To an extent, I learned to live with them, though upped my swiping when I saw fellow hikers heading down towards me, lest they draw (accurate) conclusions about my hygiene.

The path ended at a narrow, rock-covered ridge, about 400 metres above Fjordgård and 150 metres beneath the summit of Mt Hesten. At first, the incline was forgiving, and I was able to skip onwards over the rocks, but the mountain became steeper and steeper, in parts almost vertical, and I had to use my hands to pull myself through certain sections. An hour after starting the hike, a small sign came into sight at the end of a long path; it marked the top of the mountain.

The challenging route to the summit meant many made do with the view from the ridge, so when a small group left, I had the top to myself. I sat by a cliff that plummeted straight down to the ocean, half a kilometre below. Ahead, beyond the shimmering blue water, were snow-capped mountains, hazy in the sunlight. To my right and a little below, there was an enormous bowl-shaped space, its edges marked by jagged, grey ridges. It seemed like a stadium from another world, where gods might fight to the death. And to my left was Segla, casting a long shadow over Fjordgård, like the mother of all sundials.

The beauty was inescapable. For the first time during the trip, I sat in one spot for an hour, feeling the sun and the wind on my skin, and absorbing one of the most spectacular places on Earth.

The next morning, I awoke in a meadow behind a boat house. It was strewn with hay bales and old dinghies. When I had arrived the previous evening, I had been told that, due to the unusually nice weather, there was no room in the actual campsite, but I could set up in the adjoining field. As I went through the ritual of removing layers as the morning sun warmed my tent, I looked at the map. Today was the day, it seemed; from the north shores of Senja, where I now found myself, Tromsø was just 65 kilometres away.

I packed slowly, then rode slowly; I was determined to solve Arnaud's brain teaser before finishing the ride. At Botnhamn ferry terminal, I lay on a sunlit rock beside the ramp, thinking about the people in hats that had occupied my mind for the last week. When the ferry drifted into sight, an answer came to me; *yes*, I thought, *that has to be it*. I composed a response and pressed send as the ferry docked.

Drinking coffee, I gazed fondly at the water through the ferry windows. Then it hit me; this ferry would be my last. I was both sad and excited.

On the other side, on the island of Kvaløya, I saw my first sign for Tromsø. Kvaløya was no more magnificent than anywhere else in Norway – same old fjords, same old mountains – but the landscapes captivated me more than ever. Although I had seen the country change in subtle ways over the trip, whether the hues of the water or the angles of the earth, there had always been fjords and there had always been mountains. The result was that this Norway felt just like the Norway I had landed in a month ago, back when I was all clean shaven and ambitious. The country seemed like an old friend; in fact, we were new friends but the type that had travelled together, that had seen each other at the their best and at their worst. *It's true*, we said, *the depth of friendships can't be measured in days.*

Fond memories floated through my mind. The astonished looks on the faces of Trolltunga hikers upon seeing a man with a loaded bike high up in the mountains; moments on ferries when I was happy to be moving north from the comfort of a lounge; pitching my tent in the wild and the accompanying sense of freedom; the subtle 'isn't-this-great?' expressions of my fellow cyclists; and times when I basked in the idea that *this* was reality, not life at home, and that it was always there waiting for me.

I thought about the hard times too. About the cold and rain, the damp clothes, the dank tent, the climbs and the insects, how big Norway had looked on the map. I thought back to my first night when, on a depressing track beside the road, I first met the little bastards, who had swarmed me as I tried hopelessly to adjust my gears on my upside-down bike. Of course, all these moments made the present that much sweeter.

I thought about how the mountains would still be there long after I'd gone – after I'd gone home and after I'd gone gone. A thousand cyclists had ridden this road before me and a thousand more would after me. And still the mountains would be there, watching, their timelessness illuminating the brevity of our lives and spurring us to see the world while we can.

Then, pulling me from my musings, Tromsø appeared across the water, sprawled beneath a panorama of shining white mountains. *Well, there it is,* I thought, a smile on my face, *the Capital of the Arctic.*

I awoke the next morning to the beep of my phone, which lay on the grimy floor of my tent, next to my face. A new message. I stuck out a heavy hand and grabbed it. 'That's correct!' said the screen. I squinted at it. The message made no sense to my sluggish mind. I rubbed my eyes and squinted some more, then finally discerned that it was Arnaud. I grinned and let my hand fall to the cold floor. Another beep. 'So… ready for the difficult version?' *God, no.* 'Not now,' I said, 'but I'll be in touch when I next hit the road.'

I munched on some bread and cheese, then climbed out of my tent. There were other tents dotted around the woods, but it was quiet. Just the babbling of a crystal stream. My bike was leant against a tree. I patted it on the saddle as I plodded past. *Not today, old boy.*

I continued along peaceful suburban streets until I made it to the jewel in Tromsø's crown: the Arctic Cathedral, snow-white and triangular, overlooking the long bridge to the island of Tromsøya where the city centre lies. I bought a ticket and wandered in, then spent a few minutes among the polished wooden pews, admiring the blue stained glass. An old man with white hair smiled at me, then looked uneasy when he saw my trainers, which had all but fallen apart. *Yes, I know, I'm on my way to replace them now.*

Wind roared across the bridge. On the other side, ferries and cargo ships lined the shore. I walked by the water until I came to a mall, where the warm air was filled with the scents of waffles. It was my mum's birthday in a few days, so I picked up some trinkets from a souvenir shop. After, I found a shoe shop, where I bought a new pair and some socks. 'Got a bin?' I asked the girl. She picked one up and held it out. Her nose twitched as I dropped in my tattered trainers and soggy socks. Then I pulled on my fresh attire and strode towards the exit.

I had a flight to catch.

Troms Statistics

- Distance (trip total): 198 kilometres (2,333 kilometres)
- Climbing (trip total): 3,135 metres (29,580 metres)
- Highest point: 556 metres (Mt Hesten)
- Island Rides project distance: 4,817 kilometres
- Island Rides project climbing: 49,464 metres

Useful Information and Links

Seasonal road closures

Many roads, especially those in the mountains, are closed in the colder months due to ice and snow. For this reason, you often see barriers at the bottom of ascents in Norway. I was there in summer, so the roads were always open, but many would have been closed a few months earlier. If considering a trip through Norway, bear in mind the season might dramatically affect your options. Here are a couple of sites that can help with route planning:

https://www.nasjonaleturistveger.no/en

https://www.vegvesen.no/en/Home

Google Maps is also useful and seems to account for seasonal closures, though doesn't know which tunnels cyclists can and can't use. (See below.)

Tunnels

Cyclists are not permitted to use many of Norway's tunnels. For a map of which tunnels can and can't use be used, along with comments from cyclists, check out the following page, which is indispensable when planning your route through Norway:

https://www.cycletourer.co.uk/maps/tunnelmap.shtml

A note on tunnels on Senja: Although many are in a poor state of repair, a positive is that some have a special button for cyclists at their entrances. When pressed, these activate lights outside the tunnel that let motorists know there's a cyclist inside. Apparently, outside some of Senja's tunnels, there are even boxes containing fluorescent vests.

Camping

Camping in the wild is permitted in Norway, though there are a few restrictions. For example, you can't be within 150 metres of a house, you can't stay in the same place more than two nights (except in very remote areas), and campfires aren't allowed in or near forests between April 15th and September 15th. Most of the rules are common sense, though more information can be found here:

https://www.visitnorway.com/plan-your-trip/travel-tips-a-z/right-of-access/

If you feel like a break from wild camping, 100–150 kroner (US$10–15), plus a little extra for a shower token, is typical for no-frills campsites, the type that have everything you need – toilets, showers, kitchens – but that might be a little rough around the edges. Occasionally, I made the mistake of venturing into a 'nice' campsite – with fancy card-activated showers, views I was too tired to appreciate, and functioning locks on the toilet doors – and paid twice as much.

Arnaud's Bran Teezars

Bran Teezar 1

You have nine identical-looking objects – bowls, let's say – and a pair of balance scales (the type where you put something on one side and something on the other and see which is heavier). One bowl, however, is heavier than the rest. If you can only use the scales twice, how can you find out which is the heaviest bowl?

Bran Teezar 1 Solution

Put three bowls on each side of the scales. If one side goes down, the heavier bowl is among those three. If not, it's among those you didn't put on the scales. Next, take two of the three potential bowls and put them on each side of the scale. If one bowl goes down, that's your bowl. If not, it's the one you didn't weigh.

Bran Teezar 2

There are three people standing in a line. The person at the back (Person 1) can see the two in front; the person in the middle (Person 2) can see the person at the front; and the person at the front (Person 3) can't see anyone. Each is wearing a hat, either black or white. The hats were taken from a bag containing three black hats and two white black hats. The people are asked to figure out what colour their own hat is. Person 1 says they don't know; Person 2 says the same. Hearing this, Person 3 says what colour their hat is. What colour is it and how did they know?

Bran Teezar 2 Solution

If Person 1 had seen two white hats, they would have known that theirs was black. Therefore, Person 1 must have either seen two black hats or a black hat and a white hat. Person 2 realises this – that their own hat and the hat of Person 3 can't both be white. So, if the hat of Person 3 were white, Person 2 would know that their own hat is black. Since Person 2 says that they don't know the colour of their own hat, they must see that Person 3 is wearing a black hat. Person 3 realises this.

Bran Teezar 3

Twenty people are placed in a room. Each is wearing a hat, either black or white, and each has to say what the colour of their own hat is. No other communication is permitted. That is, the only thing one can say is, 'The colour of my hat is black/white.' However, before entering the room, they're allowed to discuss tactics – they can agree that 'The colour of my hat is black/white' is code for something. What code could they use and how many people will it allow to correctly guess the colour of their own hat?

Bran Teezar 3 Solution

Everybody will see an even number of one colour and an odd number of the other. Therefore, the people can agree that, if the first person to speak says, 'The colour of my hat is white,' this means they see an even number of white hats and an odd number of black hats. They would say this if, for instance, they saw 10 white hats and 9 black hats. Ignoring the hat colour of the person who spoke first, anyone wearing a white hat would see nine white hats (an odd number). And since they know the person who spoke first saw an even number of white hats, they would infer that their hat must be white. The same logic applies to anyone wearing a black hat. Therefore, everybody except the person who speaks first is able to say what the colour of their own hat is.

Rolling back to the base of Trolltunga.

Camping by a lake in Odda.

On the coast of Sognefjord, the 'King of Fjords'.

Storfjord, where landslides caused tsunamis in 1731 and 1934.

Storseisundet Bridge, Atlantic Ocean Road.

Crossing Helgeland Bridge, Leirfjord.

Hamnøy, Lofoten.

Henningsvær football pitch, Lofoten.

Bleik, Andøya.

View of Mt Segla from Mt Hesten, Senja.

End Notes

1   The nearby Knivskjellodden peninsula is actually 1.5
     kilometres further north, but is inaccessible by road. It and
     the North Cape are both on the island of Magerøya. The
     northernmost point of mainland Norway (and Europe) is
     Cape Nordkinn, about 70 kilometres east and 5 kilometres
     south.

2   Most shops close on Sundays, including supermarkets.
     Petrol stations, however, remain open.

3   With a population of just 50,000, Alesund is the 9th biggest
     settlement in Norway.

4   The maelstrom (whirlpool) referred to by Ahab is
     Moskstraumen, at the southern tip of Lofoten.

5   Arnaud gave me three 'bran teezars', which are included at
     the end of the book, should you find yourself on the road in
     need of mental stimulation.

Printed in Great Britain
by Amazon

64152301R00071